JAPAN
REDISCOVERED

Photography by **Masaharu Uemura**　　　Foreword by **Donald Richie**
Text by **Hiroyuki Irifune**

IBC
PUBLISHING

Published by
IBC Publishing, Inc.
Ryoshu Kagurazaka Bldg. 9F, 29-3 Nakazato-cho
Shinjuku-ku, Tokyo 162-0804, Japan
www.ibcpub.co.jp

Photographs by Masaharu Uemura
Text by Hiroyuki Irifune
Cover Design by Hiroyasu Murofushi
Book Design by Kenji Okazaki

Acknowledgements
The author wishes to thank the following people for the translation and proofreading of the text of this book:
Joseph Dean
Nancy Fix
Mitsuyuki Irifune
James Robert Magee
David Trevil

All rights reserved. No part of this book may be reproduced in any form without written permission from the publisher.

First Edition 2008
Second Printing February 2013

© 2008 Masaharu Uemura
All rights reserved. No part of this book may be reproduced in any form without written permission from the publisher.

ISBN978-4-89684-679-9

Printed in Japan

FOREWORD

One of the earliest foreign travelers said that Japan was like an oyster. To open it was to kill it. Well, Japan has now been opened for over one hundred and fifty years and, indeed, much has been killed. Old Japan, as it was, has been destroyed, incorporated, or gentrified. Still, like the oyster, Japan is resilient and there are still many places which retain things as they were.

It is these which Masaharu Uemura set out of documents, taking a whole year, the traditional complete four seasons, to do so. He wanted, as he has said, to discover (or rediscover) the distinct cultures of the many districts into which Japan is divided. In the face of a Japan increasingly homogenized – one form of destruction – he wanted to celebrate the many differences which also distinguish this archipelago – those which were, in his terms, still culturally alive.

They included some rather famous sites, those with which the earliest travelers had been familiar. Kyoto's Golden Pavilion is, for example, here. It is not, however, seen as another tourist sight. In his pictures of this famous building, as in all the photos in this book, Uemura has sought to return to these remains something of their original context.

This may take some doing – cropping out the Coca-Cola signs, as it were – but the result is that things reemerge rediscovered: Horyuji as it was (and occasionally is) with not a tourist in view; that much-snapped sight, the Great Buddha in Nara's Todaiji, photographed through the grill of the temple itself to return to this image something of the power and awe it once possessed.

Of course it is not the foreign tourists who opened the oyster and killed the culture. This was accomplished by the Japanese themselves as they unlocked their gates, reached out and, almost indiscriminately it would seem, dragged in things from abroad. The cultural eco-system was at once upset.

Mountains were razed, forests felled, coasts concreted, and the land developed within an inch of its life. Old buildings were either destroyed or else brought up to date. Yet there still exists a bit of Kyoto in that new, contemporary city which might as well be called Kyoto Land.

What prevents Japan from completely becoming a theme park is that the original culture is so old and so extraordinarily rich that it is not to be completely obliterated by a handful of developers. As Uemura discovered, and as he teaches us, there are still ways through which old Japan may be rediscovered.

It is a matter of selection, of focus, of attention. One learns to see not only spatially but temporally as well. Japan may be relatively small but it is in time enormous. We can, through Uemura's lens, look back to a Japan which both was and also remains. Through these pictures we can see both context and continuity.

It is to be hoped that this disclosure does not bring a new generation of developers, oyster-knives in hand. Rather, it is anticipated that it will bring a new respect what is different, unique, singular – for it is cultural plurality and not culture similarity that makes for richness.

Donald Richie

CONTENTS

FOREWORD 3

Kinki Region 6
Hokuriku and Chubu Regions 22
Kanto and Tokai Regions 42
Chugoku Region 54
Shikoku Region 66
Kyushu and Okinawa Regions 74
Tohoku Region 84
Hokkaido Region 110

A Guide to Japan Rediscovered 121
List of the Plates 132

近畿地方

Kinki Region

With Kyoto at its center, the cultural heart of Western Japan is the Kinki Region. As one of the longest inhabited areas, it is no exaggeration to say that Japanese history and the history of the Kinki Region are one and the same.

For many years this region was the home of the Imperial Family and the place where unification was first brought about in Japan. The capital was Nara. Later the capital was relocated to Kyoto and lasted until the 17th century. Nara was the center of the Buddhist religion and the capital of Japan until the 8th century. Kyoto is also where, for 1,200 years, the culture of nobility was refined with a truly Japanese focus.

The areas of Ise and Kumano prospered with their focus on religious activities, and even today, Japanese from all over Japan come to visit famous shrines or to participate in Shinto religious ceremonies and festivals.

1 Morning view of Yakushiji Temple (Nara City, Nara)

奈良 | Nara

2 The Mantoro lanterns of Kasuga Taisha (Nara City, Nara)

3 Horyuji Temple (Ikarugacho, Nara)

4 The Great Buddha in the Daibutsuden of Todaiji Temple (Nara City, Nara)

5 The Omizutori Fire Festival at Todaiji Temple's Nigatsudo (Nara City, Nara)

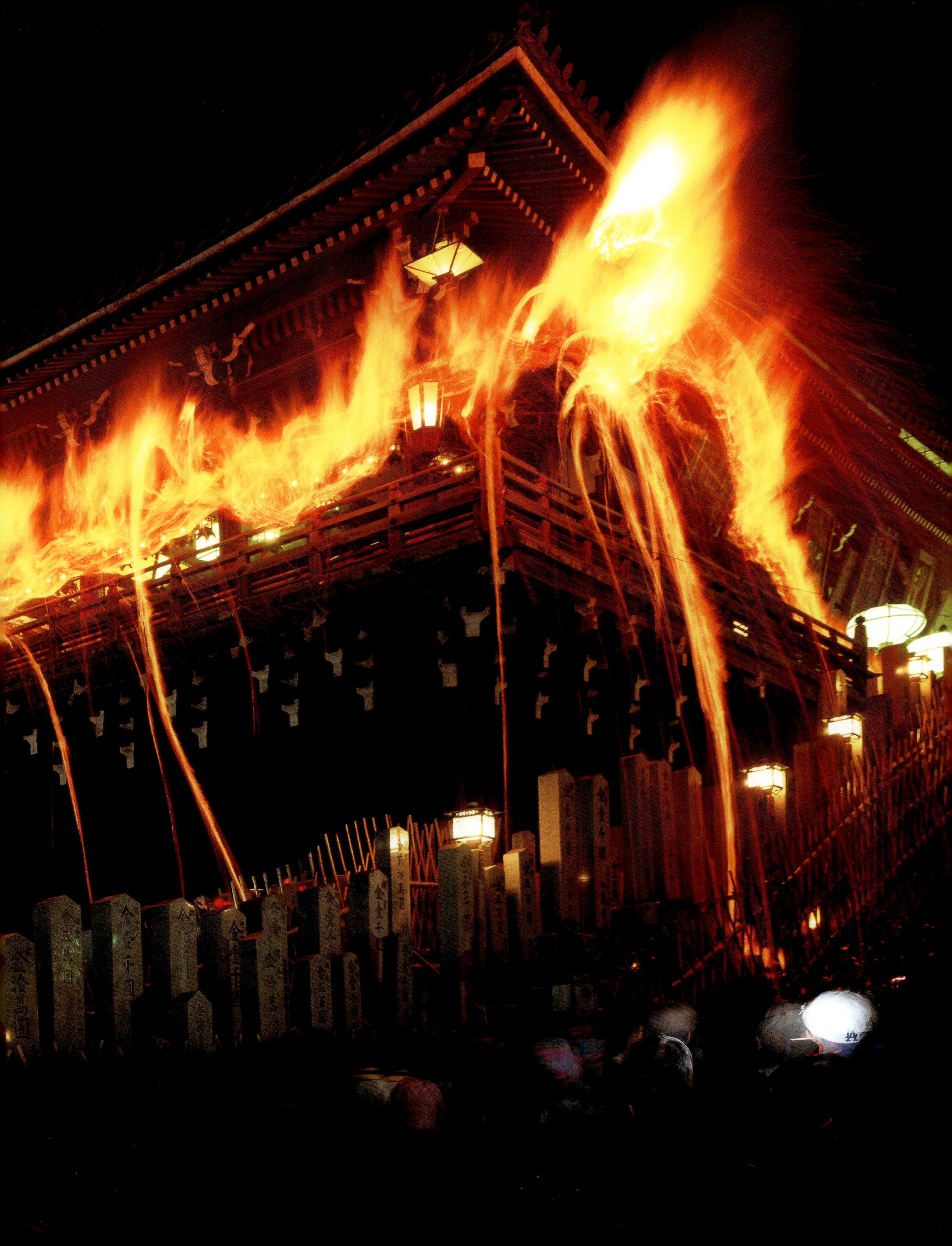

京都 | Kyoto

6 The Aoi Festival (Kyoto City, Kyoto)

7 The Aoi Festival (Kyoto City, Kyoto)

8 The Golden Pavilion (Kinkaku) of Rokuonji Temple (Kyoto City, Kyoto)

京都の石庭 | Rock Garden Minimalism

9 The Daisen-in rock garden at Daitokuji Temple (Kyoto City, Kyoto)

11 The rock garden at Ryoanji Temple (Kyoto City, Kyoto)

10 The Ryugen-in rock garden at Daitokuji Temple (Kyoto City, Kyoto)

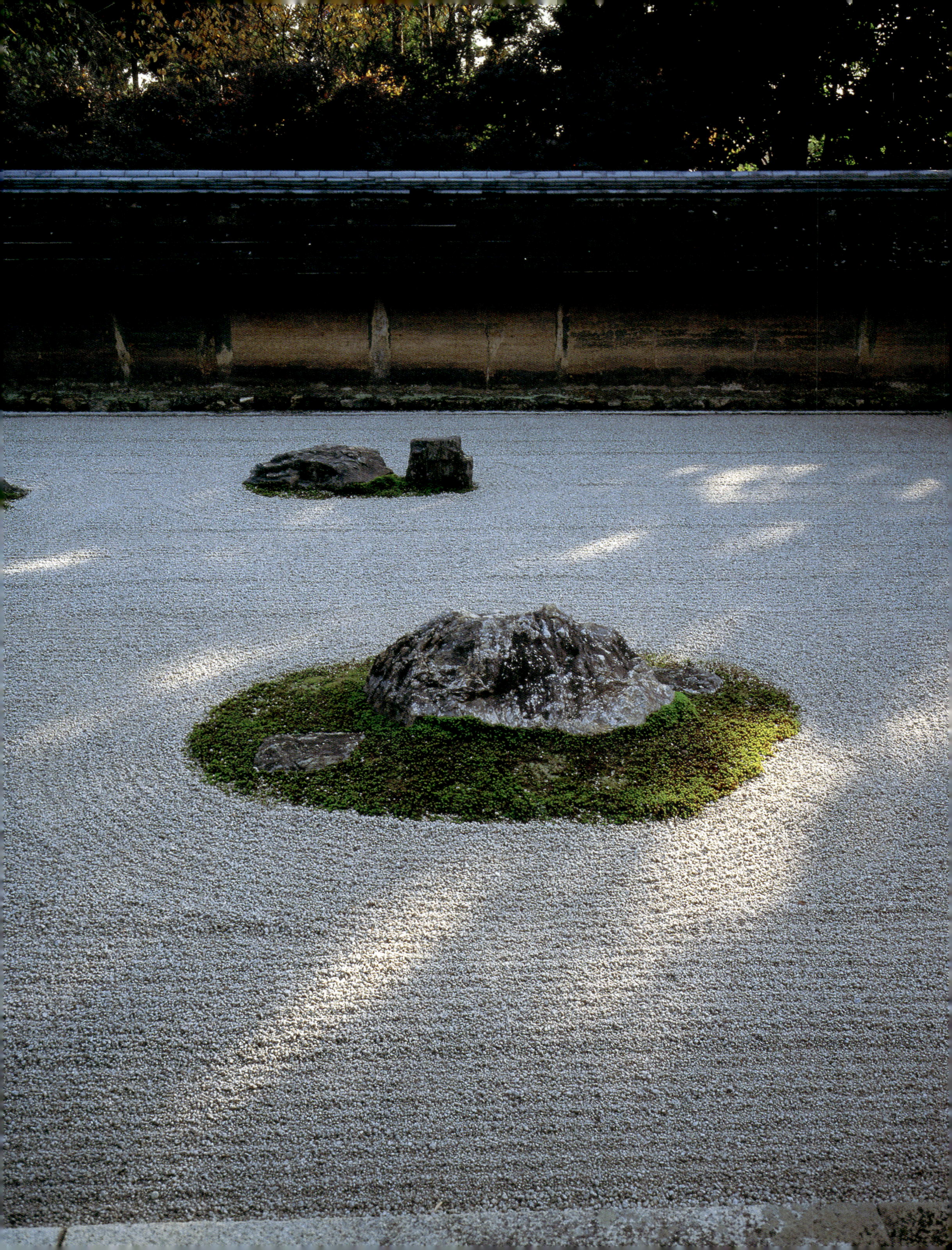

伊勢 | Ise

12 The Ujibashi Bridge at Ise Jingu Shrine (Ise, Mie)

13 The Nuiho Festival at Jingu Kanda (Ise, Mie)

14 The Otauesai (Rice Planting Festival) at Izawa no Miya (Isobecho, Mie)

長浜・近江八幡

Nagahama and Omi Hachiman

15 The Old Nishikawa House (Omi Hachiman, Shiga)

16 Children's Kabuki, part of the Hikiyama Festival (Nagahama, Shiga)

熊野 | Kumano

17 The Nachi Falls (Nachikatsuuracho, Wakayama)

18 The three-storied pagoda of the Seigantoji Temple (Nachikatsuuracho, Wakayama)

19 The Nachi no Himatsuri Fire Festival at Nachi Taisha (Nachikatsuuracho, Wakayama)

20 The Oto Festival at Kamikura Jinja (Shingu, Wakayama)

北陸・中部地方

Hokuriku and Chubu Regions

The Hokuriku and Chubu Regions are located in the central part of Japan, and contain a mix of both the Western and Eastern Japanese cultures.

In the Chubu Region, the Japan Alps, the most prominent mountain range of the country, are a popular refuge from the heat of the lower lying areas in the summer, and in the winter, provide world class skiing opportunities. The southern portion of this area is a strategic location for transportation and prospers with its granary facilities. To the north, extremely large snowfalls have given rise to a "*yukiguni*" or "Snow Country" culture. During the Warring States period in the 16th century, this area was a point of Japanese unification.

The Hokuriku Region to the north, faces the Japan Sea and was heavily influenced by the colorful culture of Western Japan. This region is especially well known for its unique lacquerware and porcelain products.

21 An open hearth at Kita House (Nonoichimachi, Ishikawa)

22 Kenrokuen Garden (Kanazawa, Ishikawa)

金沢 | Kanazawa

23 Noh Theater (Kanazawa, Ishikawa)

24 Kita House (Nonoichimachi, Ishikawa)

福井 | Fukui

27 Lush green at Eiheiji Temple (Eiheijicho, Fukui)

25 Moss garden at Heisenji Temple (Katsuyama, Fukui)

26 The Sanmon Gate of Eiheiji Temple (Eiheijicho, Fukui)

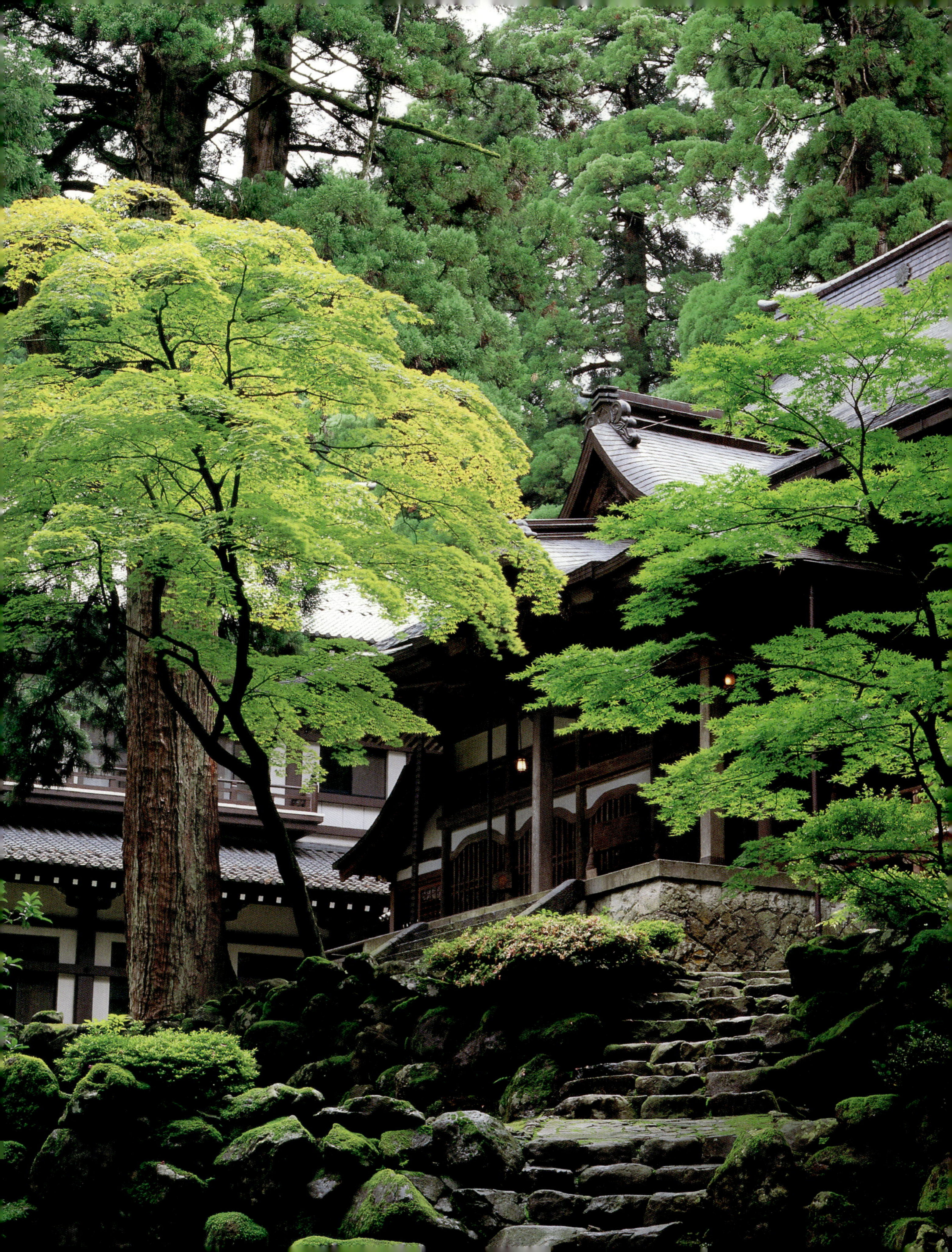

高山 Takayama

28 Traditional homes line a street in Takayama (Takayama, Gifu)

29 Cherry trees in bloom line the Miyakawa (Takayama, Gifu)

30 Elaborate *karakuri ningyo* (puppets) of Takayama Matsuri (Takayama, Gifu)

飛騨の民家

Traditional-style homes of Hida

31 The Old Mishima House (Shokawamura, Gifu)

33 The Old Kusakabe House (Takayama, Gifu)

32 The Yoshijima House (Takayama, Gifu)

白川郷 | # Shirakawago

34 *Koi-nobori* (carp streamers) and the Iwase House (Kamitairamura, Toyama)

35 The *Doburoku* (home-brewed sake) Festival (Shirakawamura, Gifu)

36 A community of *gassho-zukuri* (hands-clasped-in-prayer) homes (Shirakawamura, Gifu)

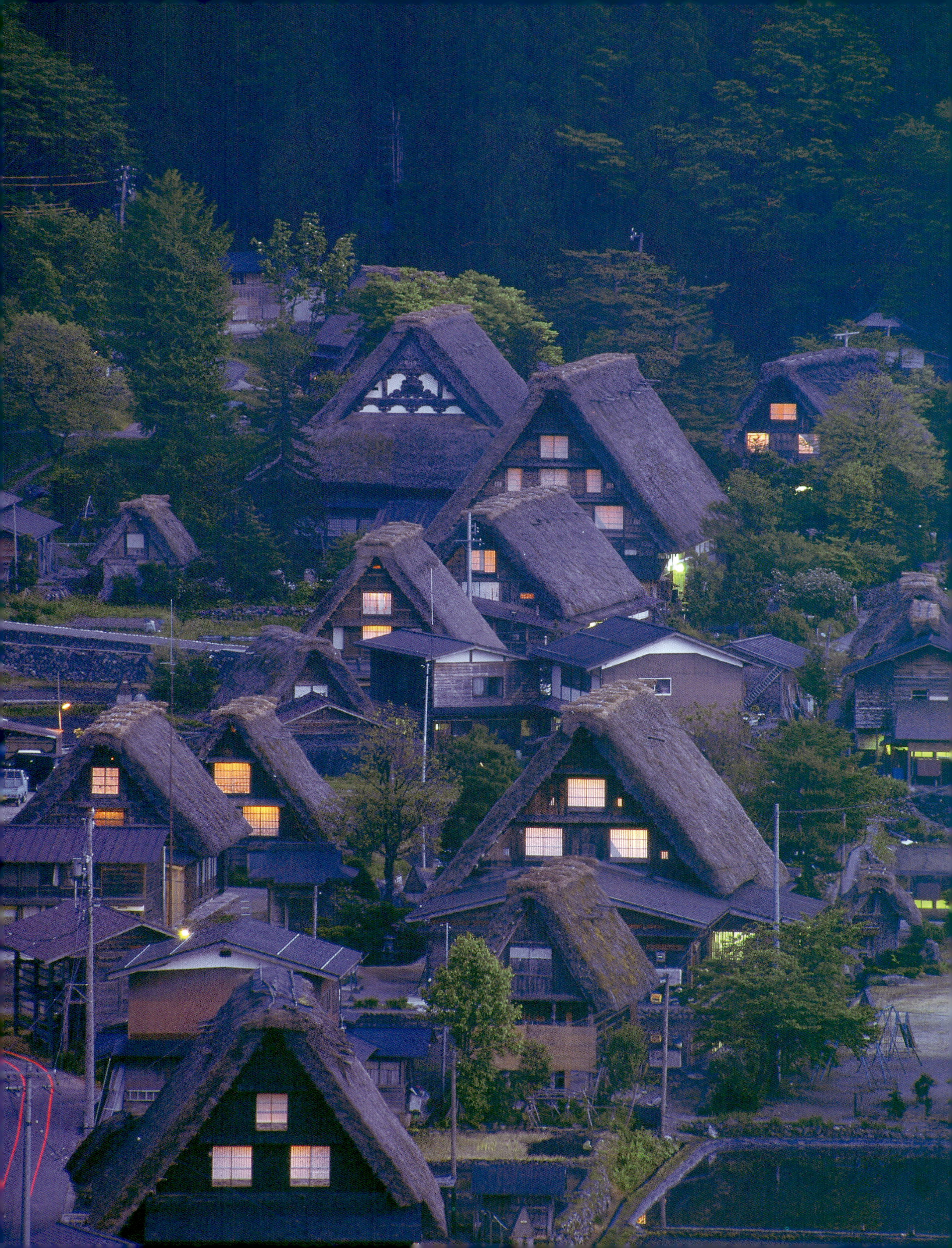

遠山郷 | Toyamago

37 The Shimotsuki Festival (Kamimura, Nagano)

38 The Shimotsuki Festival (Kamimura, Nagano)

39 The Shimotsuki Festival (Kamimura, Nagano)

木曽路 Kisoji

40 Naraijuku (Narakawamura, Nagano)

41 An inn in Otsumago (Nagisomachi, Nagano)

42 An open hearth in Waki-Honjin-Okuya (Nagisomachi, Nagano)

長野
Nagano

43 A stone Buddhist image at Manji (Shimosuwamachi, Nagano)

44 Zenkoji Temple (Nagano City, Nagano)

大垣 | Ogaki

45 *Setsubun* at Hokoin's Hidarime Fudo (Ogaki, Gifu)

46 The Hidarime Fudo Hadaka Matsuri at Hokoin (Ogaki, Gifu)

47 Swans on Lake Hyoko (Suibaramachi, Niigata)

瓢湖

Lake Hyoko

48 Swans on Lake Hyoko (Suibaramachi, Niigata)

地獄谷温泉
Jigokudani Onsen

49 Monkeys in snow (Yamanouchimachi, Nagano)

50 A monkey in a spa (Yamanouchimachi, Nagano)

関東・東海地方

Kanto and Tokai Regions

The centrally located Kanto and Tokai Regions face the Pacific Ocean and have a temperate climate. In the Kanto Region is located Japan's largest plain which is also the location of the metropolis of Tokyo. In the past, Tokyo, known as "Edo," was the seat of the Tokugawa Shogunate which functioned as Japan's capital for 300 years, starting in the 17th century. In the 19th century, the Emperor moved to the city, which officially became the capital, Tokyo.

On the outskirts of Tokyo are several towns where the atmosphere of the Edo period survives. The shrine of the Tokugawa Shogun is located in Nikko, and in addition to being a famous tourist attraction, is designated as a World Heritage Site. The old capital of Kamakura, located in Kanagawa Prefecture, flourished in the 13th century and retains the atmosphere of its past glory.

The "Tokaido Road" connecting Tokyo with Kyoto was the source of great prosperity in the Tokai Region. Located on this road were fifty-three relay stations, which flourished thanks to the travelers who passed through. But today, there are few stations that retain traces of the past. The ever present and majestic Mt. Fuji is one of the remnants of this route.

51 The *taisai* (Great Festival) of Nikko Toshogu (Nikko, Tochigi)

52 The Three Monkeys of Toshogu (Nikko, Tochigi)

日光 | Nikko

54 The ornate Yomeimon Gate of Toshogu (Nikko, Tochigi)

53 The Nikko Sennin Gyoretsu Procession (Nikko, Tochigi)

44

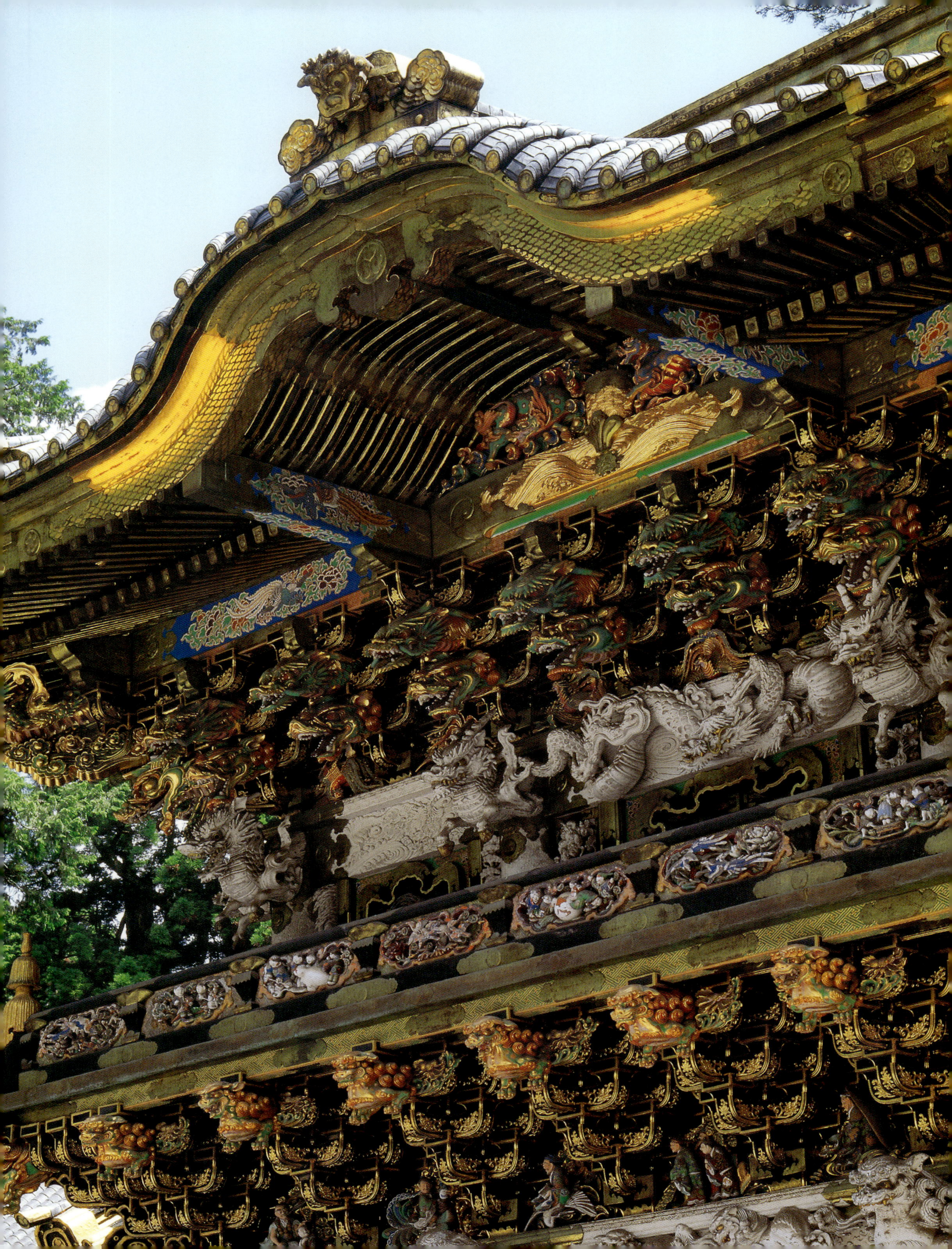

秩父 | Chichibu

55 Chichibu Yomatsuri (Night Festival)
(Chichibu, Saitama)

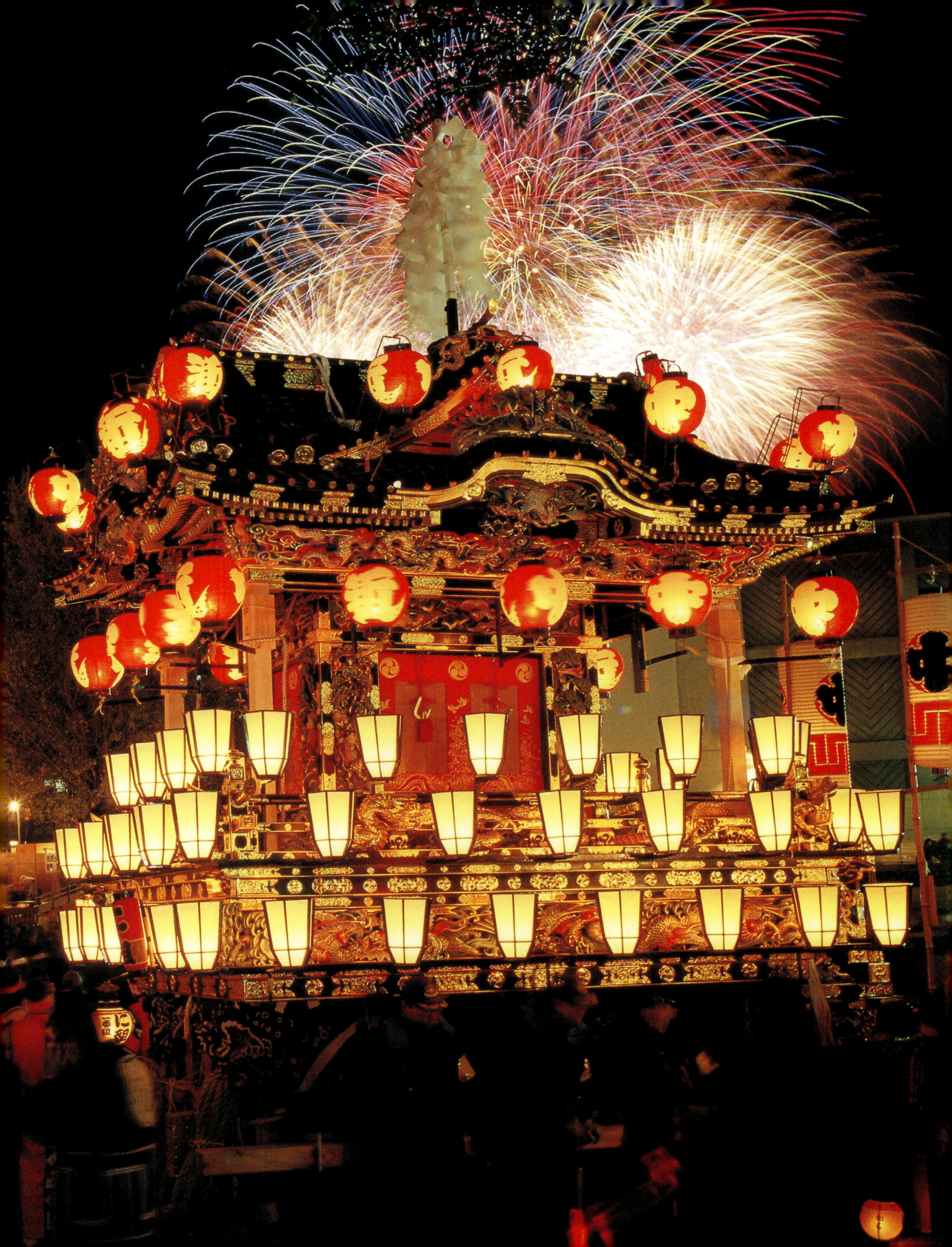

川越

Kawagoe

56 *Kura-zukuri shoka*, the traditional fireproof home of a merchant (Kawagoe, Saitama)

57 The 500 Disciples of Buddha, stone images, at Kitain (Kawagoe, Saitama)

58 The Kawagoe Matsuri (Kawagoe, Saitama)

59 The Great Buddha at Kamakura (Kamakura, Kanagawa)

鎌倉 | Kamakura

60 Tsurugaoka Hachimangu (Kamakura, Kanagawa)

61 *Yabusame*, mounted archers perform at the Tsurugaoka Hachimangu (Kamakura, Kanagawa)

62 Sunset viewed from Lake Motosu-ko (Kamikuishikimura, Yamanashi)

富士山
Mt. Fuji

63 Mt. Fuji and Lake Yamanaka (Yamanakakomura, Yamanashi)

東海道
The Tokaido

64 Ohashiya Lodge at Akasakajuku (Otowacho, Aichi)

65 Ohashiya Lodge at Akasakajuku (Otowacho, Aichi)

中国地方

Chugoku Region

Long ago, before Eastern Japan appeared on the stage of Japanese history, situated between the regions of Kinki and Kyushu, was the "Middle Country," or in Japanese, "Chugoku" Region.

Mountains separate the Chugoku Region into the "San-in" and "Sanyo" areas on the Japan Sea and Seto Inland Sea sides, respectively. The Sanyo area has busy economic activities and has had a lot of traffic since the old days, and there remain many castles and houses of wealthy merchants. On the other side of the mountains, the San-in area has prospered through its fishing industry.

The Chugoku Region is the origin of many ancient legends, including that of an independent kingdom in the Izumo region of San-in. In Sanyo are ancient tumuli, or royal tombs, which are on the same scale as those found in Nara. These are the source of many unique events and customs.

66 Izumo Taisha (Taishamachi, Shimane)

67 The *shinba* (sacred horse) of Itsukushima Jinja (Miyajimacho, Hiroshima)

68 The five-storied pagoda of Itsukushima Jinja (Miyajimacho, Hiroshima)

宮島 | Miyajima

69 The *otorii* (Great Sacred Gate) at Itsukushima Jinja (Miyajimacho, Hiroshima)

岩国 | Iwakuni

70 Kintaikyo Bridge (Iwakuni, Yamaguchi)

瀬戸内海

Seto Naikai – Japan's Inland Sea

71 Dawn breaks over the Inland Sea from Mt. Fudekage (Mihara, Hiroshima)

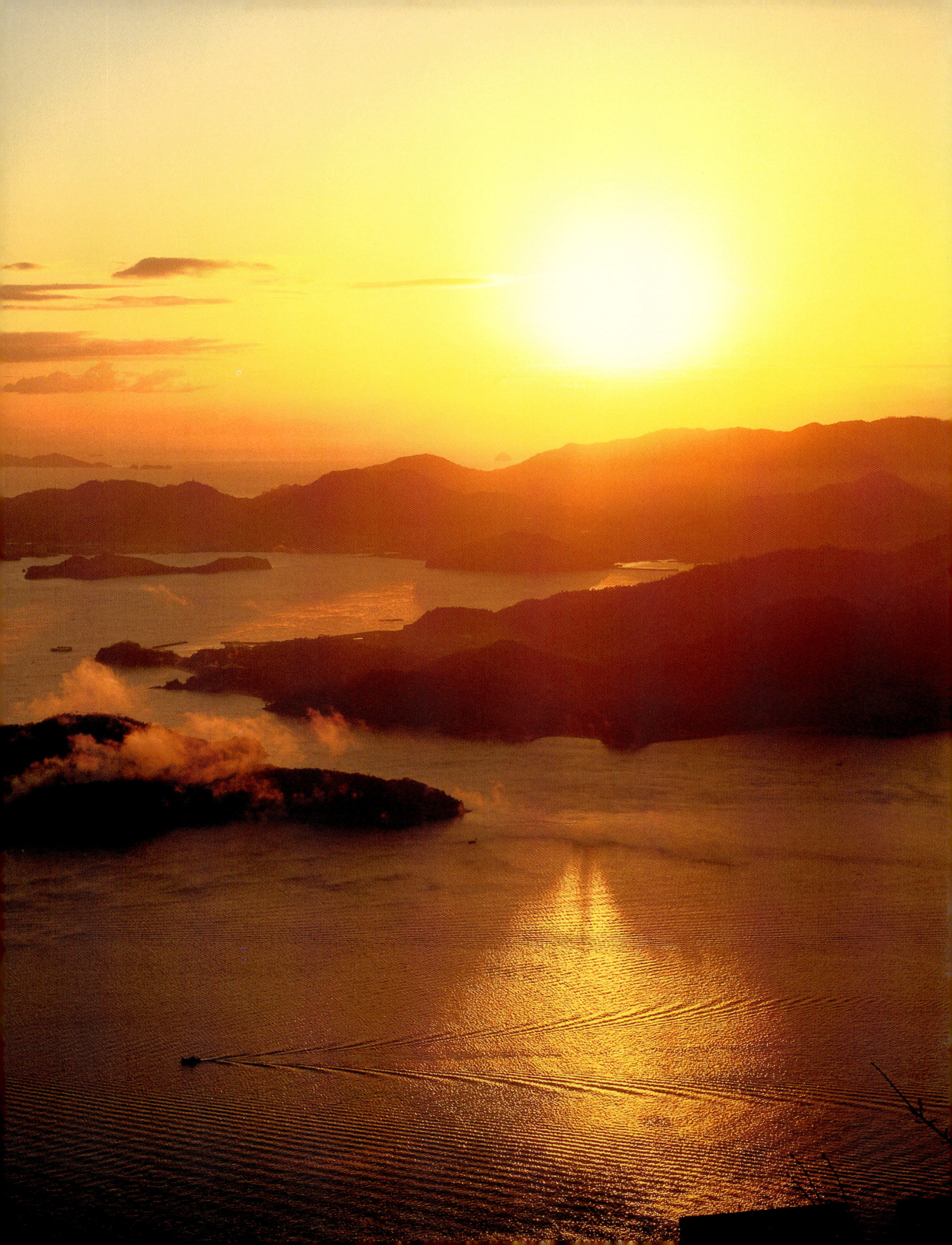

Merchant Houses in Sanyo

山陽の商家

72 The Old Katayama House (Nariwacho, Okayama)

73 The Matsuzaka House (Takehara, Hiroshima)

倉敷
Kurashiki

74 A museum dedicated to the building of traditional Japanese storehouses (Kurashiki, Okayama)

75 A scenic canal at Kurashiki (Kurashiki, Okayama)

津和野
Tsuwano

76 A canal running beside traditional samurai homes (Tsuwanocho, Shimane)

77 The *sagi-mai* (White Heron Dance) (Tsuwanocho, Shimane)

78 Himeji Castle colored by the sunset (Himeji, Hyogo)

姫路 | Himeji

79 Inside Himeji Castle (Himeji, Hyogo)

備中
Bicchu

80 The five-storied pagoda in Kibiji (Soja, Okayama)

81 The night dances of Bicchu (Biseicho, Okayama)

64

82 The Hadaka Matsuri at Saidaiji Temple (Okayama City, Okayama)

岡山
Okayama

83 Okayama Castle (Okayama City, Okayama)

四国地方

Shikoku Region

Shikoku or "four countries" derived the name from the fact that in the distant past, the region was divided into four different nations. The island of Shikoku is separated from the main Japanese island of Honshu by the Seto Inland Sea and falls under the cultural influence of Western Japan. The climate of Shikoku is temperate and the Pacific coast of the island weaves up and down. Shikoku's central area is mountainous and still boasts many natural areas. There are now three major bridges connecting Shikoku to Honshu and access to this area by highway has become quite easy. In recent years, Shikoku's development has progressed rapidly, but it is hoped that Shikoku can retain its traditional Japanese atmosphere.

During the Edo period, it was quite common for pilgrims to make the "Grand Tour" of 88 temples of Shikoku, and even today, there are many Japanese who at least once in their lifetime, will try to make this journey on foot.

84 Kazurabashi Bridge (Nishi-iyayamason, Tokushima)

徳島
Tokushima

85 A performance of Awa Ningyo Joruri (Tokushima City, Tokushima)

86 A performance at Jurobe no Yashiki (Tokushima City, Tokushima)

87 The Awa-odori dance (Tokushima City, Tokushima)

88 *Ema* (votive tablets) at the Emado, Kotohiragu Shrine (Kotohiracho, Kagawa)

香川
Kagawa

89 An engineering marvel, the Seto Ohashi Bridge (Sakaide, Kagawa)

90 Marugame Castle (Marugame, Kagawa)

70

91 Ritsurin Park (Takamatsu, Kagawa)

92 Kami-Haga-tei (Uchikocho, Ehime)

93 Latticework at Hon-Haga-tei (Uchikocho, Ehime)

内子 Uchiko

94 The Uchiko-za Theater (Uchikocho, Ehime)

松山 | # Matsuyama

95 Dogo Onsen (Matsuyama, Ehime)

九州・沖縄地方

Kyushu and Okinawa Regions

Kyushu is the southernmost of Japan's main islands, and has a unique culture and customs. It is also said that the stubborn nature of its "male society" goes against the mainstream, which may be the reason why so many Kyushu samurai in the area have been actively involved in past revolutions.

The port of Nagasaki in Kyushu, being the closest geographical point to the Asian continent, was the sole open door to the outside world during the period of isolation of the Edo period (1603~1967).

Kyushu is also famous for its many active volcanoes, which lend a mysterious aura to the landscape, and have been the origin of many Japanese legends.

Okinawa
In the far south of the Japanese Archipelago and away from the main Japanese islands is Okinawa. Because of its location, it has been influenced by both Japan and the Asian continent, giving rise to a very unique culture. It is also one of the most diverse areas of Japan with a myriad of customs and dialects used on the islands.

96 The stern face of the Usuki Stone Buddha (Usuki, Oita)

長崎 | # Nagasaki

97 The Peiron Boat Race (Nagasaki City, Nagasaki)

98 Oura Tenshudo (Nagasaki City, Nagasaki)

99 Nagasaki at dusk (Nagasaki City, Nagasaki)

桜島
Sakurajima

100 A volcanic eruption at Sakurajima (Kagoshima City, Kagoshima)

飫肥 | Obi

101 Obi Castle (Nichinan, Miyazaki)

102 A flume of an old samurai residence (Nichinan, Miyazaki)

知覧
Chiran

103 An old samurai residence (Chirancho, Kagoshima)

104 An old samurai residence (Chirancho, Kagoshima)

阿蘇 Aso

105 The Onda Matsuri (planting festival) of Aso Jinja (Ichinomiyamachi, Kumamoto)

106 The Onda Matsuri (planting festival) of Aso Jinja (Ichinomiyamachi, Kumamoto)

銀鏡
Shiromi

107 A Shiromi Kagura performance (Saito, Miyazaki)

沖縄 | Okinawa

108 The sun goes down on Nagura Bay (Ishigakijima, Okinawa)

109 Traditional homes of Taketomijima (Taketomijima, Okinawa)

110 The Tanetorisai (Taketomijima, Okinawa)

東北地方

Tohoku Region

Not having been fully opened up until the 9th century, the Tohoku Region is rich in tradition and culture. The Tohoku Region is situated in the north of the main Japanese island of Honshu, and, in the past, was connected to Edo by the Oshu Highway. On the northern coast on the Pacific Ocean side are cliffs often pounded by storms, and in the central mountains, three to four meters of snow is common.

The Japan Sea side of this region is famous for its granaries, and from spring to summer this area boasts some of Japan's most fertile terrain. In the fall, throughout the Tohoku Region, festivals are held to welcome the season in the hope of bountiful harvests. Many of the festivals have a long tradition and exhibit the vibrant local customs and performing arts.

111 Harvested rice (Zao, Yamagata)

112 The Nishimonai Bon Odori dance (Ugomachi, Akita)

東北の夏祭り | # The Summer Festivals of Tohoku

113 A Tanabata Picture lantern (Yuzawa, Akita)

114 The Nishimonai Bon Odori dance (Ugomachi, Akita)

115 Aomori's Nebuta Matsuri (Aomori City, Aomori)

青森菱友会

116 Great towers of lanterns at Akita's Kanto Matsuri (Akita City, Akita)

東北の冬祭り | # The Winter Festivals of Tohoku

117 Kamakura, small snow scene (Yokote, Akita)

118 Hiburi Kamakura, Fire Festival (Kakunodatemachi, Akita)

南会津
Minami Aizu

119 A row of thatched houses in Ouchijuku (Ouchijuku, Fukushima)

120 Hinoemata Kabuki (Hinoematamura, Fukushima)

121 Tajima Gion Festival (Tajimamachi, Fukushima)

会津
Aizu

122 A farmhouse with a traditional storehouse in Sugiyama District (Kitakata, Fukushima)

123 A farmhouse with a traditional storehouse in Sugiyama District (Kitakata, Fukushima)

124 The Nanokado Hadaka-mairi (Yanaizumachi, Fukushima)

松島
Matsushima

125 A festive ship in the Shiogama Port Festival (Shiogama, Miyagi)

126 Matsushima's Godaido Hall (Matsushimacho, Miyagi)

127 A shrine in the Hote Matsuri (Shiogama, Miyagi)

出羽 | Dewa

128 The villager and the multi-level homes of Tamugimata (Kushibikimachi, Yamagata)

129 Kurokawa Noh performed at Kushibikimachi (Kushibikimachi, Yamagata)

130 The five-storied pagoda of Mt. Haguro (Haguromachi, Yamagata)

131 The Jodo-style garden of Motsuji Temple (Hiraizumicho, Iwate)

平泉

Hiraizumi

132

The *noh-mai* dance of Chusonji Temple (Hiraizumicho, Iwate)

133 The Shishi Odori (Hiraizumicho, Iwate)

134 A farmhorse (Tono, Iwate)

135 A traditional *magariya* (Tono, Iwate)

遠野 | Tono

136 Remains of the Hayachine pilgrimage trail (Tono, Iwate)

137 Hayachine Kagura, traditional entertainment (Ohasamamachi, Iwate)

138 The storehouse of a traditional warrior's residence (Kakunodatemachi, Akita)

角館
Kakunodate

139 A traditional warrior's home (Kakunodatemachi, Akita)

140 The front gate of the Aoyagi House (Kakunodatemachi, Akita)

141 A snowy street in front of a traditional warrior's house (Kakunodatemachi, Akita)

弘前
Hirosaki

142 The 500 wooden disciples of Buddha at Choshoji Temple (Hirosaki, Aomori)

143 Hirosaki Castle and cherry trees in bloom (Hirosaki, Aomori)

144 An ornate float in the Neputa Matsuri (Hirosaki, Aomori)

東北の自然 | # The Natural Beauty of Tohoku

145 Kuroyu of Nyuto Onsenkyo (Tazawakomachi, Akita)

146 Sukayu Onsen (Mt. Hakkoda, Aomori)

147 The beautiful Oirase River (Towadakomachi, Aomori)

北海道地方

Hokkaido Region

The northernmost point of Japan is Hokkaido, which is only one island but comprises an entire region. While winters are extremely cold, Hokkaido has no rainy season and a very mild comfortable climate. Hokkaido is blessed with an abundance of nature, including a variety of wild flora and fauna.

Large-scale development of Hokkaido did not begin until the 19th century when "pioneers" from all over Japan came and settled in this vast and beautiful region. Large Western style dairy farms lend a European or American feel to the landscape, and in the major cities of Hakodate and Sapporo, Western culture seems to have taken root, often giving the impression of being in a foreign country.

The Ainu, an indigenous people of Japan, once lived throughout Northern Japan, but were gradually pushed north through Japanese encroachment in Hokkaido. It was commonly thought that the Japanese were a homogeneous race, but this idea is currently being challenged.

148 Swans at Akan National Park (Akan National Park, Hokkaido)

函館 | Hakodate

149 A Russian Orthodox Church (Hakodate, Hokkaido)

150 Night view of Hakodate (Hakodate, Hokkaido)

札幌
Sapporo

151 Christmas at Odori Park (Sapporo, Hokkaido)

アイヌ | Ainu

152 Lake Onneto (Akan National Park, Hokkaido)

153 The Marimo Festival (Akancho, Hokkaido)

154 Ainu people (Akancho, Hokkaido)

北海道の冬
A Hokkaido Winter Scene

155
Tancho cranes in
mating dance
(Tsuruimura, Hokkaido)

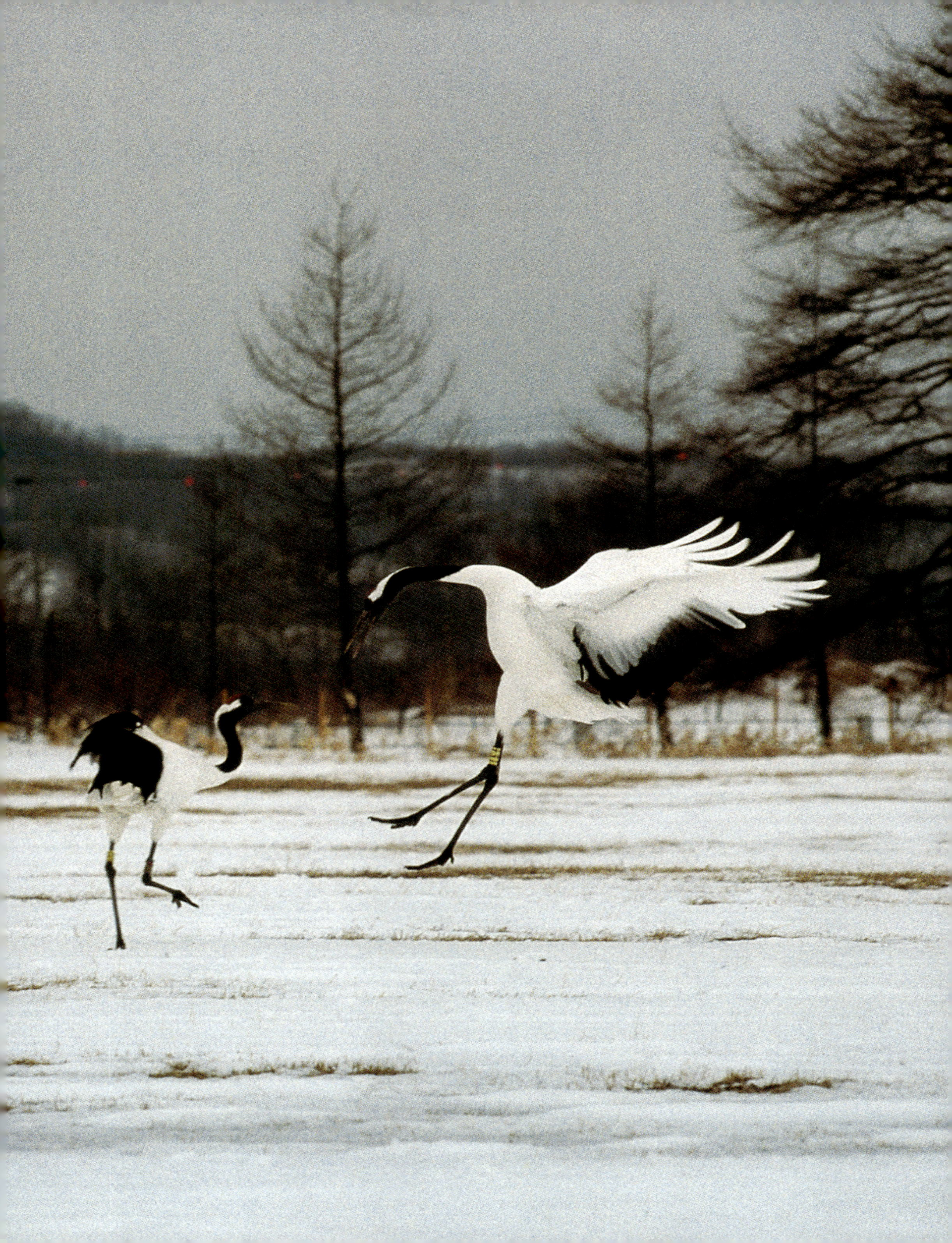

156 Ice floes off the Sea of Okhotsk (Utoro, Hokkaido)

157 Sunset in Okhotsk (Utoro, Hokkaido)

158 Port Utoro in winter (Utoro, Hokkaido)

A Guide to Japan Rediscovered

Kinki Region

1. Nara

From the year 710 to 784, Nara was the capital of Japan where seven generations of emperors firmly established the beginnings of the nation. This capital was, at the time, called "Heijokyo" and was modeled after the Chinese capital of "Choan." In fact, the Tang Dynasty of China exerted great influence, and through the establishment of a Chinese style bureaucracy and a Buddhist inspired aristocracy, the "Tenpyo Culture" of Nara thrived. This area became what can be called the easternmost point of the Asian Silk Road. Many magnificent works of art reflecting the culture of this period survive and are open to the public at Nara's temples and museums.

Todaiji Temple and the Great Buddha
The most important symbol of Nara, Todaiji Temple is located in Nara Park. Passing through the Nandaimon Gate, the visitor will encounter the "Daibutsuden," the Hall of the Great Buddha. This is considered the world's largest wooden statue of Buddha and twice every year the windows of the Daibutsuden are opened for public viewing of the Great Buddha's face. ▶ 4

Omizutori at Nigatsudo
In addition to the overwhelming scale and grandeur of this historical area, every March the Buddhist event of "Omizutori" is held at the Nigatsudo portion of Todaiji Temple. In this event, eleven Buddhist priests run through Nigatsudo carrying giant wooden torches. The festival is intended to welcome spring and pray for a plentiful harvest. With the Year 2002, this ceremony will have taken place 1,250 times since its commencement in the 8th century. ▶ 5

Horyuji Temple
Constructed in the early 7th century, Horyuji Temple, is the world's oldest wooden structure and was Japan's first World Heritage Site. The five-storied pagoda is reflective of the Asuka Culture of that time. ▶ 3

Mantoro Matsuri
The Mantoro Matsuri is a festival of fire which takes place every winter and summer in the Corridor of the Kasuga Taisha Shrine, in which 3,000 hanging lanterns are lit. This shrine holds the guardian deity of the historic Fujiwara Clan, and it is said that the lanterns were lit every night in the prosperous days of this family. ▶ 2

Yakushiji Temple
Yakushiji Temple was originally constructed in Kyoto at the end of the 7th century by the Emperor Tenmu, who commissioned it in order to pray for his ailing Empress. This temple is famous for the rhythmical beauty of its East and West pagodas and its cathedral-like construction. In the Year 710, Yakushiji Temple was moved with the relocation of the capital to Nara. ▶ 1

2. Kyoto

With 1,200 years of history, Kyoto is the cultural heart of Japan. It is difficult to express, in a few pages, the contrast of exquisiteness and simplicity that Kyoto offers.

Exquisite Kyoto and the Aoi Festival
The Aoi Festival is one of the three major festivals in Kyoto, and every spring this event seeks to reenact in splendid detail the Royal Court of the 9th century Kyoto. Participants representing the Heian period imperial household dress in the exquisite kimonos worn by military and civil servants, and conduct a procession that includes decorated ox carts and umbrellas.
▶ 6, 7

Kinkaku Rokuonji Temple
At the end of the 14th century this building was constructed by the Shogun, or ruling general, Ashikaga Yoshimitsu. This three-storied building was covered with gold leaf and after the Shogun's death became a temple representing the "Kitayama Culture." The Kitayama Culture represents the dual elements of simple samurai tradition and sophisticated culture of royal nobility.
▶ 8

3. Rock Garden Minimalism

Rock gardens are constructed of arranged moss-covered rocks to express the feeling of islands in a sea of white sand. They are disarmingly simple in that they do not use plants as other gardens. This type of garden can be found at Zen temples throughout Japan, with the rock gardens at Ryuanji and Daitokuji temples in Kyoto, especially famous. The geometric designs of rock gardens might be considered to be the predecessors of some forms of modern art.
▶ 9, 10, 11

4. Ise

Ise is one of the Japanese Shinto religion's holiest places. It is a typical Shinto belief that after death, Japanese emperors do not go to the Buddhist paradise, but rather remain in Japan as gods. The place where these ancestors of the Imperial Household inhabit is said to be the Ise Jingu Shrine. Ever since the 14th century pilgrims have been visiting this holy site, and in the Edo period (17th to 19th centuries) it was a source of status for a pilgrim to have completed the pilgrimage known as the Grand Tour with a visit to Ise.
▶ 12

All over Japan, religious ceremonies are held to pray for prosperity and good harvests but the ceremonies at Izawa no Miya and Ise Jingu Shrines are especially prestigious.

The Otauesai Rice Planting Festival of Izawa no Miya
For over 2,000 years, this festival has been celebrated, regardless of the weather, with a young girl planting rice sprouts in the fields.
▶ 14

The Nuiho Festival of Ise Jingu Shrine
In the Ise Jingu Shrine, there is a ricefield dedicated solely to the use of the gods and is the focus of the Nuiho Festival. First, after the shrine's Shinto priests form a long line, an offering of newly harvested rice is made to the sun goddess. Then the "Niinamesai," or Shinto harvest festival commences.
▶ 13

5. Nagahama and Omi Hachiman

Nagahama and Hikiyama Festival
The decorated float towed in a shrine's festival is known as a dashi and was once considered to be the soul of a kami, or god. Another kind of structure is the palanquin-like mikoshi, or portable shrine, the vehicle for the soul of the gods. As time passed, the mikoshi became the central part of the festival, and as the towns sponsoring festivals grew in prosperity; the dashi became more and more ornate as a form of competition between towns to symbolize their wealth.
▶ 16

The Hikiyama Festival of Nagahama was first begun in the latter half of the 16th century when the lord of Nagahama Castle gave a present of gold to the village people as a way of celebrating the birth of his son. Using this gold, the village people were able to make a very ornate dashi and today, there are twelve of these hikiyama dashi remaining. As part of this festival, there is the "Children's Kabuki" which is performed entirely by children under twelve years old.

Omi Hachiman and the Old Nishikawa House
Omi Hachiman, facing Lake Biwa, is a merchant town brought to prosperity through its canals. Originally the residence of a prosperous "Omi merchant" it was constructed in the first part of the 18th century. The Old Nishikawa House has been designated as an Important Cultural Property. This mansion was built in the Kyoto style, but the character of an efficient merchant can be seen throughout.
▶ 15

6. Kumano

The Kumano Region, with its high concentration of prestigious jinja or Shinto shrines, is known for its religious beliefs. One of these many shrines is the Kamikura Jinja, where every February is held the festival of fire called the "Oto" Festival. In this festival, some 2,000 men will hold torches made from pinewood and run down a stone stairway making it look like a waterfall of fire. This is a festival for men to test their bravery and on the day of the race women are strictly forbidden from entering the mountain where the festival is held.
▶ 20

Nachi Fire Festival
Every July at the most famous shrine in Kumano, "Nachi Taisha," the Nachi Fire Festival is held. After a traditional Japanese dance called dengaku is performed in the shrine's inner sanctuary, men carrying large pinewood torches will wave them violently, with sparks and flames scattering about. The ritual is aimed at testing the endurance and bravery of the participants as they descend to the bottom area of the waterfall.
▶ 19

Nachi Falls and Nachi Seigantoji Temple
Of the many mountain waterfalls in Japan, at 133 meters, the Nachi Falls are certainly the most famous. Facing these falls is the famous temple of Nachi Seigantoji, and dominating the landscape is Kumano's famous landmark and symbol, the three-

storied pagoda. This area is the starting point for those who make the pilgrimage of Western Japan's 33 famous temples.
▶ 17, 18

Hokuriku and Chubu Regions

1. Kanazawa

Until the 19th century, Kanazawa was ruled by the Maeda Clan, which because of its economic strength was constantly eyed suspiciously by the central bakufu, or feudal government. Since then, the castle tower has been torn down and at one time the interior was used as a location for a university campus. Today, throughout the town, many magnificent cultural treasures remain.

Kenrokuen Garden
One of the three most beautiful traditional gardens in all of Japan is "Kenrokuen." This garden is famous for the way tree branches which are supported in preparation for the heavy winter snows, the two-legged Japanese lanterns and Japan's oldest fountain. From the lookout tower can be seen a panoramic view of the castle-town. ▶ 22

Noh Theater
This area is also famous for its gorgeous lacquerware, pottery and contribution to traditional arts. Since the Edo period, the Japanese "Noh" theater has been a tradition of pride for the local people and in Kanazawa, Noh performances are still held regularly. ▶ 23

Kita House
In the suburbs of Kanazawa, there remains the Kita House designated as an Important Cultural Property for its northern or "Hokuriku" style architecture. The Kita House was originally the home of the Kita family who ran a distillery, and the house was built in the traditional way with earthen floors and open fire hearths. ▶ 21, 24

2. Fukui

Eiheiji Temple
The main temple of the Soto Zen School, a major sect of the Buddhist Zen religion, is Eiheiji Temple, which is located in serene and beautiful mountains. This temple has a history of some 750 years and is still a retreat for many Buddhist followers who come to study the strict Soto teachings of Dogen Zenji. As one of the most prominent figures of Japanese Buddhism, Dogen Zenji taught the practice of shikantaza, or sitting in spiritual contemplation, and the philosophy of banishing worldly goods.
▶ 26, 27

Heisenji Temple
Two kilometers away down a cedar-lined mountain path lie the moss covered ruins of Heisenji Temple. In the distant past, the area surrounding this temple was ruled by an organization of warrior priests, but in the latter half of the 16th century, Heisenji was destroyed in a peasant uprising and all that remains is a small and simple sanctuary. ▶ 25

3. Takayama

Takayama is a town in the snowy mountains of Hida, and the town is often called "little Kyoto." It developed as a castle town by Kanamori Nagachika in the 16th century. It thrived with crafts and is famous for wooden handicrafts. Merchant houses in the Edo period still remain in the center of the city. The area is preserved for its historical buildings. ▶ 28, 29

Takayama Matsuri
Takayama Matsuri is a famous festival held twice a year in the spring and summer. It is a traditional event that has been continuing since the beginning of the 18th century. Festival floats called yatai attract many people to this mountain town. Each yatai is uniquely decorated but the one named modoshi guruma with the wind-up dolls is the crowd favorite. The wind-up puppetry is proof of the high level of craftsmanship achieved in the modern age of Japan. ▶ 30

4. Traditional-style Homes of Hida

Yoshijima House and Old Kusakabe House
The Yoshijima House of Takayama City is famous for adapting the Edo period architecture to local conditions by cleverly using wooden beams vertically and horizontally to distribute evenly the weight of heavy winter snows. The result is a house, which incorporates not only the functional logic of scientific thinking but also a home, which is extremely beautiful. Next door to the Yoshijima House is the Old Kusakabe House. When these two houses were being built, their respective carpenters competed to make structures which are now designated as two of Japan's Important Cultural Properties. ▶ 32, 33

Old Mishima House
In the village of Shokawa, the Old Mishima House, built in the mid-18th century, used 300 cypress trees in the construction and is a country manor which sets the standard of homes in the Hida area. Great effort has been taken to preserve the library and sunken hearth in this structure. ▶ 31

5. Shirakawago Village

In the past this area was uncharted and used as a place where people were exiled from society. Then at the end of the 12th century, a group of samurai, who had suffered defeat in battle, moved into the area and created the Shirakawago Village.

Gassho-zukuri Houses
The severe cold and heavy snow of this area gave rise to the peculiar gassho-zukuri or literally "praying hands" shaped houses named after the 60 degree angled roofs which are made in the shape of hands clasped in Buddhist prayer. This type of unique but extremely functional dwelling was first described in the famous German architect Bruno Taut's 1939 book, "Rediscovering Japanese Beauty." Today there are some 100 of these dwellings that are still used as residences and in 1999, the houses were registered collectively as a World Heritage Site. ▶ 36

Doburoku Festival
Every October in Shirakawago Village, the "Doburoku Festival" is held to celebrate the local harvest. The villagers perform the lion-dance around each of the homes and enjoy drinking the unrefined home-brewed sake rice wine called doburoku, from which the festival takes its name. ▶ 35

6. The Shimotsuki Festival of Toyamago Village

Toyamago Village in the Ina Valley was another remote area and even today is off the beaten path. For this reason ancient customs and folklore still remain. In the middle of December the harvest festival of "Shimotsuki" is held with the parishioners of the local shrine celebrating with traditional dance and Shinto music throughout the night. The next morning, the purification ceremony of "Yutate-shinji" is held with water being boiled over a furnace and then sprinkled on the participants exemplifying a ritual of purification. ▶ 37, 38, 39

7. The Lodging of Nakasendo, Kisoji

Deep in the mountains, along the Kiso Road, a part of the Nakasendo highway, the two lodging villages of "Tsumago" and "Narai" beckon travelers.

Tsumago
The village of Tsumago was established as a place of lodging by the military government of the Edo Bakufu in the early 17th century when the national highway system was constructed. The highway system stretched from Nihonbashi in Edo (present-day Tokyo) to points all over Japan. Tsumagojuku is one of the lodging villages of the Nakasendo and this portion of the national highway has been chosen by the Ministry of Education as a Preservation District for Groups of Historic Buildings. One of the famous lodges in Tsumagojuku is "Tsutamuraya" at Otsumago, one of the areas in the village; formerly a farmhouse known for the size of the pillar which supports the building's roof. ▶ 41

Waki-Honjin-Okuya
In times past, lodging reserved for high-ranking members of society such as the daimyo, feudal lords was called a honjin. A waki-honjin was another lodging used to compliment the honjin when extra service was required. Lodging towns used to have quarters for both and in Tsumago, "Waki-Honjin-Okuya" is the house of a distinguished family which also functioned as a wholesale store. ▶ 42

Naraijuku
Naraijuku was another lodging town located at the entrance to Kiso, a bustling town of horse-carts and travelers, which catered to those transporting high class shipments. Today, the 19th century feeling is still evident, and it is designated for a Preservation District for Groups of Historic Buildings. ▶ 40

8. Nagano

Suwa Taisha and the Manji Stone Buddha
The Manji Stone Buddha, located near the Suwa Taisha Shimosha-Harumiya Shrine, was created from a naturally round stone in the third year of the Emperor Manji (1660) and is over 2 meters in height. ▶ 43

Zenkoji Temple
Zenkoji Temple has some 1,400 years of history and is well known for appealing to a broad range of religious sects. During the Edo period, Zenkoji Temple was one of the Grand Tour pilgrimage sites, and even today, is one of Japan's most visited temples. The principal object of worship for this temple is a statue of Buddha that arrived from India by way of the Korean Peninsula, and is the oldest object of its kind in Japan. It has not been open to public viewing since the Year 654. ▶ 44

9. Ogaki

Gifu Prefecture is located in the geographical center of Honshu, the main island of Japan, and traditionally the southern part of the prefecture focusing on Ogaki City has been an important transportation hub. The area was also of very strategic importance for national unification, and in ancient Chinese, gifu meant "crossroads of unification." In the 16th century, Oda Nobunaga, a high-ranking samurai, who was instrumental in pushing for national unification, named this area.

The Hidarime Fudo Hadaka Odori "Naked Dance" Festival
In Japan, February 3rd is the date the spring setsubun festival is held. However, at the temple of Hokoin Hidarime Fudo in Ogaki City, the setsubun festival is quite out of the ordinary. First, in order to purify themselves, the male participants will remove all of their clothes and enter the nearby river. Then, in the large arena, the men will battle to gain possession of a wooden club known as a rikenboku, all the while working up a sweat and causing steam to rise from their bodies in the bitter cold.
▶ 45, 46

10. The Swans of Lake Hyoko

Every year in Niigata Prefecture the man-made Lake Hyoko attracts wild swans that have migrated from Siberia. Because of successful feeding programs the numbers of swans seem to increase every year. ▶ 47, 78

11. The Monkeys of Jigokudani Onsen

The Northern Alps in Japan is famous for the many, well-known and secluded hot springs. Japan is the northernmost habitats of wild monkeys and those monkeys which do live in this bitterly cold climate are famous for their custom of keeping warm by jumping in and relaxing in the local hot springs. ▶ 49, 50

Kanto and Tokai Regions

1. The Shogun's Shrine, Nikko

The shrine of Tokugawa Ieyasu, the first Edo Bakufu Shogun, had been located in Mt. Kuno in the Tokai Region, but in 1617 was transferred to Nikko, near present day Tokyo. Because processions following the Shoguns was customary of visiting the shrine, the main road of Nikko flourished. The Nikko road also has the distinction of being designated a Special Natural Monument because of the ten-thousand cedar trees, estimated to be over 300 years old, which line the town's streets.

Yomeimon Gate of Nikko Toshogu
Constructed in 1634, the shrine dedicated to Ieyasu, is now called Nikko Toshogu and is representative of Japanese shrines devoted to ancestor worship. One of the most unique features of this shrine's architecture are the bronze roof tiles and brilliant coloration of the Yomeimon Gate. ▶ 52, 54

Nikko Sennin Gyoretsu
At Toshogu Shrine every spring and fall, the "Nikko Sennin Gyoretsu" procession is held. This festival reenacts the transfer of Tokugawa Ieyasu's spirit from Mt. Kuno to Nikko. This festival focuses on three mikoshi, or portable shrines, and some 1,200 people, dressed as samurai warriors, participate by walking to the entrance of the shrine. ▶ 51, 53

2. Chichibu

In the Edo period, the mountains of Chichibu were considered holy places in Musashi Province and widely worshipped. Even today, Chichibu is one of the 34 locations where pilgrims visit Japanese temples.

Chichibu Yomatsuri
Chichibu was known as a thriving merchant town where periodically, silk markets were held. This area is also well known for its lively Chichibu Yomatsuri, the night festival held every December. The six 300-year old parade floats that are part of this festival, were built without the use of even one nail, and are bathed in the light of their Japanese lanterns and fireworks from the night sky. Adding to the excitement are the residents from nearby rural towns and villages who come to participate in the traditional event. Along with the Gion and Hidatakayama Festivals, the Chichibu Yomatsuri is one of the three great festivals in Japan and was designated an Important Intangible Cultural Property. ▶ 55

3. Kawagoe

Kurazukuri Storehouses
The town of Kawagoe is famous for its kura-zukuri storehouse architecture. In the past, the kind of dignified architecture was carefully planned to reduce the possibility of fire in these storehouses and was prevalent everywhere in Edo. As Edo developed, this type of architecture gradually disappeared. However, in Kawagoe, or Little Edo, many of these old-style buildings and the atmosphere continue because of the strong economic ties with Edo. Even now, four times every day, one can hear the echo of an ancient bell used to signal time to the people of Kawagoe. ▶ 56

Kitain Temple
The ancient temple of Kitain, often called Kawagoe Daishi, is the main temple in the Kanto area of the Tendai Buddhist sect. Within the confines of this temple are the famous 500 Disciples of Buddha, "gohyaku rakan" which expresses a multitude of human expressions. From the 18th to the 19th century, 535 stone images were carved into this sculpture. ▶ 57

Kawagoe Matsuri
The most exciting time for Kawagoe is in the fall, when the Kawagoe Matsuri festival is held with huge floats being paraded through the streets. This is one of the Kanto Region's three largest festivals. ▶ 58

4. Kamakura

In the 12th century the first Shogunate, or feudal government, was controlled by the ruling samurai and formed in Kamakura. The reason that Kamakura was chosen for the seat of this government may be because that with the sea to the front and mountains to the rear, Kamakura offered the qualities of a unique natural fortress.

Tsurugaoka Hachimangu
One of Kamakura's most visible symbols is the shrine of Tsurugaoka Hachimangu, upon which construction was begun in 1063. This shrine was considered the protector of the Shogunate government and was where its members worshipped. ▶ 60

Yabusame
Today, there is still some connection between Tsurugaoka Hachimangu and the previous feudal Kamakura Government in the form of the great festival that still takes place. One event this festival offers is the yabusame, where a mounted samurai will try to ride his horse and shoot a bow and arrow at a series of small targets. For the samurai of the time, this was a typical practice exercise, then later; it developed into a sport. Today, the ritual is considered a religious event. ▶ 61

The Great Buddha at Kamakura
Another symbol of this area is, without doubt, the Great Buddha at Kamakura. Designated a National Treasure, this statue of Buddha was constructed of bronze, and the pedestal is 13.35 meters in height and weighs about 121 tons. The Great Buddha is hollow and it is possible to view the interior. ▶ 59

5. Mt. Fuji

At about 3,800 meters, Mt. Fuji is Japan's highest peak. Not being part of any nearby mountain range, the beautiful shape of Mt. Fuji towers alone above the landscape, and is honored in countless works of art and poetry. Mt. Fuji is actually a volcano, and its eruptions carved out many lakes at its foot, which formed summer resorts that attract vacationers from throughout Japan. ▶ 62, 63

6. The Lodging Stations of Tokaido Road

In the 17th century, the Tokaido Road connected the main Japanese cities of Edo and Kyoto, and on this road there were fifty-three lodging stations where travelers could rest during their journey. Today, little remains of the Tokaido Road, with the exception of the lodging town of Akasakajuku. ▶ 64, 65

Leading up to Akasakajuku is the natural landmark of rows of pine trees that extend for two kilometers giving the old road the same atmosphere of its heyday hundreds of years ago. Upon reaching Akasakajuku, one can find the spirit of the 300-year old Ohashiya Lodge, still in good condition, providing safe haven for travelers who wish to rest for the night.

Chugoku Region

1. Izumo

In the 8th century, Izumo was one of the settings mentioned in the "Kojiki" and the "Nihon Shoki" the ancient chronicles of Japan, and even today is recognized as one of Japan's historic holy locations. From ancient times this area was said to be an independent kingdom with a high level of cultural development.

Izumo Taisha
One example of common ancient Japanese architecture that still exists today is the shrine of Izumo Taisha where people offer prayers under its giant sacred straw festoon. ▶ 66

2. Miyajima

The shrine of Itsukushima Jinja on Miyajima Island is thought to have been constructed in the latter half of the 6th century, and in 1996, was registered as a World Heritage Site. In front of this floating shrine is the unique vermilion-lacquered sacred gate, or otorii which was built in the mid 12th century by Taira no Kiyomori, who in the last days of the Heian period was the ruler and one of the most famous men in old Japan. This shrine is dedicated to the guardian deity of the sea. ▶ 67, 68, 69

3. The Kintaikyo Bridge of Iwakuni

In the former stronghold of samurai culture, Iwakuni City of Yamaguchi Prefecture, there is one of the three most famous bridges in Japan, Kintaikyo Bridge. This sturdy wooden structure has a length of 193.3 meters, width of 5 meters and was built in 1673. Well known for its unique shape and solid construction, the original bridge was destroyed by a typhoon in 1950 and rebuilt in 1953. ▶ 70

4. Seto Naikai – Japan's Inland Sea

Between the main Japanese islands of Honshu and Shikoku, there are three routes, which span the Seto Naikai, or Seto Inland Sea. However, of these the one that best expresses the romantic feel of the area is the "Nishiseto Expressway (Setouchi Shimanami Kaido)." This road weaves its way through the large and small islands that dot the Seto Inland Sea with 10 different bridges, and is unique for being able to be crossed by foot or bicycle. From the top of Mt. Fudekage in Hiroshima Prefecture, the bridges of Setouchi Shimanami Kaido can be seen. ▶ 71

5. Merchant Houses of the Sanyo Area

Many Edo period merchant towns still remain on the Seto Inland Seas side of the Chugoku Region.

The Copper Mining Town of Nariwacho Fukiya
From the late Edo to the Meiji period, the town of Nariwacho Fukiya was known for its mining and manufacturing, and was a central point for the collection of ore in the Chugoku Region. In the latter half of the Showa period in 1972, the copper mines closed, and the town is now known for its buildings with ornate lattice doors that are preserved by Japan as traditional works of architecture. ▶ 72

The Salt Works of Takehara
Facing the Seto Inland Sea is the Edo period salt producing town of Takehara in Hiroshima Prefecture. This area is designated as an area of preservation because of the individuality of each house's lattice work and roof tiles. Especially famous is the early 19th century merchant home "Matsuzaka House," known for its exquisite roof and bay windows. ▶ 73

6. The Storehouse Town of Kurashiki

Kurashiki is a historic town in Okayama Prefecture that prospered as a granary area under the direct control of the Edo feudal government. Kurashiki, which literally means "storehouse," is now famous for its Edo period houses that line the town's canals and have been collectively designated as an area for architectural preservation. ▶ 74, 75

Since the Meiji period this town was also famous for its red brick textile mills, the remains of which still exist today. Many of the town's storehouses are now used as museums and other cultural purposes.

7. Tsuwano

Traditional Samurai Homes
With seven hundred years of history, the town of Tsuwano in Shimane Prefecture is known as the "Little Kyoto" of the San-in Region. The Tonomachi area of this castle town contained many samurai residences, of which many still stand today. Also remaining is a feudal clan school which from the Edo period to the fifth year of Meiji in 1872, taught military arts to the children of samurai. The school produced some of the most elite members of the feudal clan. ▶ 76

The Sagi-mai White Heron Dance
In July at the Shinto shrine of Yasaka the "Tsuwano Gion Matsuri" festival is held with the sagi-mai White Heron Dance. This ethnologically valuable event still retains the rich traditions of its beginnings when it was first brought over from Kyoto in the early 19th century, and is now designated as an Important Intangible Cultural Property. ▶ 77

8. Himeji Castle

Built as a fortress in the 14th century, Himeji Castle is known by

the nickname of "White Heron" for its elegant beauty and is the most famous castle in Japan. In the 16th century, the feudal warlord Toyotomi Hideyoshi increased the scale of this castle and in the beginning of the 17th century, the feudal lord Ikeda completed the existing five-tiered castle tower. Never once destroyed by fire, Himeji Castle remains unique and with Horyuji Temple were chosen as Japan's first World Heritage Sites in 1993. From the upper levels of the castle, the islands of the Seto Inland Sea can be seen beyond the former castle town.
▶ 78, 79

9. Bicchu

The Five-storied Pagoda of Bicchu Kokubunji Temple
Bicchu, in Okayama Prefecture, is said to have many ancient historical spots, one of which is the five-storied pagoda of the Bicchu Kokubunji Temple. The temple towers gracefully on a hill and has become the symbol of Bicchu. This pagoda is said to have been rebuilt in the 14th century, and again in the 18th century. ▶ 80

Bicchu kagura
A ritual dance of the southwest region of Okayama Prefecture is known as the Bicchu Kagura. Because the Bicchu area was independent of the ancient Japanese Imperial Court of Yamato before the 4th century, the unique beliefs and culture of the area are said to be at the root of the Bicchu Kagura tradition. ▶ 81

10. Okayama

The Hadaka Matsuri of Saidaiji Temple
The Hadaka Matsuri, or naked festival of Saidaiji Temple in Okayama City, is said to be one of the liveliest in Japan. Taking place in February, the coldest time of the year, this festival starts at midnight when two wooden sticks called shingi are thrown into the midst of some thousand men who wear only loin cloths. Those who touch the shingi are said to be bestowed with good fortune for the coming year, so competition for the shingi is fierce. ▶ 82

Okayama Castle
This jet-black castle with the nickname of "Ujo" which means "Castle of the Crow" was constructed in the 16th century in two generations of the ruling Ukita Clan. Then, just three years after its completion, the castle was confiscated by the feudal Tokugawa government, and until the Meiji Restoration in the mid 1800s was home to the Ikeda Clan. In 1945, during the Second World War, Okayama Castle was burned down, and despite being a "castle of bad luck" was rebuilt in 1966. ▶ 83

Shikoku Region

1. Kazurabashi

In the deep mountains of Shikoku, there is a legend that in 1185 the Heike Clan, which had been defeated in the battle of Yashima on the Kagawa Prefecture coast, escaped from Kyoto and came to this area to hide.

The Kazurabashi Bridge was the sole bridge crossing the Iya River, one of many mountain rivers in this area. ▶ 84

2. Tokushima

Awa Ningyo Joruri
In the Edo period, unlike some other performing arts, ningyo joruri, or puppet drama was one form of entertainment open to the general public. In Tokushima, presentations of puppet dramas took place at the Jurobe Yashiki residence, which was famous for the large-sized puppets used. The drama based on the life of an actual person, Jurobe became popular though the story was slightly different from the real history. ▶ 85, 86

Awa-odori Dance
The Awa-odori dance in Tokushima City is the most famous Bon dance in Japan and due to its lively steps which can be compared to the wild Brazilian Carnival. In the summer season of Bon, each person will do their own individual steps so that even beginners or those standing on the side can join in. ▶ 87

3. Kagawa

Kotohiragu Shrine
From the 18th to the 19th centuries, this area was well known for the Grand Tour, a religious pilgrimage of eighty-eight Shikoku temples and shrines. The shrine with the most significance on this pilgrimage was Kotohiragu. Tea houses and folk craft shops line each side of Kotohiragu's stone staircase extending 1,368 steps. From the top, a panoramic view of the Sanuki Plain, can be seen. ▶ 88

Marugame Castle
Ten kilometers from Kotohiragu is the castle town of Marugame City. It was here where the generations of daimyo overlords ruled. The three-tiered and stonewalled Marugame Castle tower is famous for its beauty and workmanship. ▶ 90

Ritsurin Park
Next to the Marugame area ruled by the Marugame Clan was the Takamatsu Clan, rulers of the former nation of Sanuki. In the 17th century, the leader of this clan ordered the beginning of construction of Ritsurin Park, which for five generations of rulers was added onto and improved until its completion in the 18th century. With its ancient pine trees and its fifteen beautifully constructed bridges, Ritsurin is one of Japan's "Famous Three" parks. ▶ 91

4. Uchiko

Hon-Haga-tei and Kami-Haga-tei
Uchiko is a small town in the mountains of Ehime Prefecture that has very well preserved the atmosphere of the Edo period. The houses of wealthy merchants that made their fortune through wax and paper production still remain. The houses of the Haga family, for example, are separated into the main family home (Hon-Haga) and the branch family (Kami-Haga) home. Both are designated as National Important Cultural Properties, and the Kami-Haga house is open to the public as a "Wcx Memorial Hall." ▶ 92, 93

Uchiko-za Theater
At the Uchiko-za Theater can be seen Kabuki plays and traditional dramatization of Edo period life. This theater has been designated as an Important Cultural Property for its traditional Edo-style architecture. ▶ 94

5. Dogo Onsen

This is one of the most famous hot springs, onsen in Japan. Dogo Onsen is also a favorite of Japanese writers and is often the setting for their novels. The symbol of the Dogo Onsen area is the Onsen Honkan, a public bathhouse constructed in 1894. This grand wooden structure still maintains the feel of the Meiji period. ▶ 95

Kyushu Region

1. The Usuki Stone Buddhas

The 59 stone Buddhas of Usuki City in Oita Prefecture have been designated a National Treasure. For a thousand years these statues have withstood wind and rain ever since they were chiseled into the face of a cliff from the 9th to 12th centuries. The finest statue, the Dainichi Nyorai image, suffered a broken head which has since been repaired and returned to its original state. ▶ 96

2. Nagasaki

From the 17th to 19th centuries, Japan was in a period of self-imposed isolation, shut off from the outside world with the exception of the port of Nagasaki. The federal government allowed Nagasaki to remain open as the trading post with Holland and China. From this "open port" not only were many new items from Asia and Europe imported into Japan, but also many concepts of western knowledge which contributed greatly to Japan's successful modernization. Holland was an especially important contributor in this respect as well as China, which contributed festivals and a variety of foods. ▶ 99

Oura Tenshudo
In the Edo period, Christianity was forbidden and those who practiced that faith were dealt with harshly. However, even with the threat of severe punishment, many refused to give up their faith and began to practice in secret as kakure or hidden Christians. Later, in the Meiji period, the ban on Christianity was lifted and the local Westerners built the Oura Tenshudo, a cathedral made of wood and designed in the Gothic style.
▶ 98

The Peiron Boat Race
Nagasaki was greatly influenced by the Chinese, many of whom crossed over to Japan bringing with them their cuisine and lively festivals. One such festival is the Peiron Boat Race where the participants race in Chinese-style boats called peiron which comes from the Chinese word meaning "white dragon." This event was introduced by the Chinese in 1655 and is the highlight of every Nagasaki summer. ▶ 97

3. Sakurajima

Sakurajima is an active 1,117-meter volcano located on the innermost part of Kinko Bay and because of a recent eruption that filled the ocean with lava, is now connected to the Osumi Peninsula. A mere five kilometers away on the opposite shore of the bay is the former castle town of Kagoshima City near to the volcano that frequently emits large quantities of smoke and ash.
▶ 100

4. Obi

On the hill above the town of Obi in Nichinan City in Miyazaki Prefecture is Obi Castle, in which stands the historically significant Otemon Gate. Near Obi Castle is the district of Maezuru where former samurai residences line the streets of the town. ▶ 101, 102

5. Chiran

The town of Chiran on the Satsuma Peninsula in southern Kyushu known as Satsuma's Little Kyoto still holds strongly to the traditions of the past samurai society. Here we find the Edo samurai residences and seven beautiful gardens. The gardens are designated as National Places of Scenic Beauty. Along the main road of the town are former samurai residences lined with southern-style ishigaki or stone fences. This area was chosen as an important Preservation District for Groups of Historic Buildings. ▶ 103, 104

6. The Onda Matsuri of Aso Jinja

Mt. Aso is the world's largest caldera-type volcano, and in the crater some seventy thousand people live. Also here is the Shinto shrine of Aso Jinja where every July the planting festival of the Onda Matsuri is held. In this festival women dressed in white carry offerings to the gods above their heads as they walk through the lush green of the summer rice fields. ▶ 105, 106

7. The Shiromi Kagura of Miyazaki Prefecture

Miyazaki is where many Japanese legends were first formed, and is famous for its mysterious looking landscapes and traditional performing arts. In the Shiromi area of Miyazaki the Shinto shrine of Shiromi Jinja was constructed in the 15th century. At the yearly grand festival held at this shrine every December is held the very rare Shiromi Kagura performance which depicts an ancient hunt and takes place in a simple garden setting in the center of four oak trees. This festival is held in the hope of making a successful wild boar hunt, and because of its rarity was made an Important Intangible Cultural Property in 1977. ▶ 107

8. Okinawa

Separated from the main Japanese islands, the Okinawa islands in the south of Japan were an independent kingdom up until the 16th century and thus have a variety of unique customs and features like the coral reefs of the Yaeyama Islands which are not found anywhere else in the country. ▶ 108

Tanetorisai at Taketomijima
On Taketomijima can be found the traditional Okinawan village with ishigaki, stone fences, and houses with red tile roofs adorned with shisa guardian lions, which are thought to have magical powers. Every November on this island is held the "Tanetorisai" Festival which contains a mix of Japanese and Chinese influences. All of the island's inhabitants participate in the hope of having an abundant harvest. ▶ 109, 110

Tohoku Region

1. Rice Harvest in Yamagata

In early autumn, in preparation for threshing, rice stalks are bundled and dried in what is one of Japan's rustic rural scenes.
▶ 111

2. The Summer Festivals of Tohoku

The Nishimonai Bon Odori Dance of Ugomachi, Akita Prefecture
In Japan, July or August 15th is the o-bon or summer solstice season, a time when people believe the spirits of their ancestors return to the world of the living. Around this time, people will return to their hometowns to celebrate a variety of events and festivities welcoming the return of their ancestors. ▶ 112, 114

In the Nishimonai Bon Odori dance of Ugomachi in Akita Prefecture, the single women adorn themselves in black hoods, while married women participate in the festival wearing flower-decked hats. All the women wear the traditional patchwork hanui isho kimono that is often handed down from mother to daughter. Singers and musicians will accompany the women playing the Japanese flute or shamisen, a three-stringed guitar, and drums. The songs that are performed are local favorites with a comical flair that evoke laughter from the spectators. The songs and festivities praying for abundant harvests leave a lasting impression and remind people that the summers in this northern region are far too short.

The Tanabata Picture Lantern Festival of Yuzawa
In Japan, on the 7th of July or August, "Tanabata Day" is staged throughout the country and festivals are held in celebration. In Yuzawa City in Akita Prefecture, the Tanabata Picture Lantern Festival is held annually. In this festival, Japanese garden lanterns are painted with images of beautiful women and hung throughout the city. It is said that a princess who married into a local family from Kyoto decorated strips of colored papers to evoke memories of her home, a custom, which grew into the Lantern Festival. ▶ 113

The Kanto Matsuri of Akita
Every August in Akita City, the summer festival of kanto (bamboo pole lanterns), is held. This festival is unique in that 46 lanterns weighing some 50 kilograms are attached to the top of bamboo poles which measure over ten meters long. Participants hold the poles upright on the palms of their hands or heads in a competition of balance. ▶ 116

The Nebuta Matsuri of Aomori
The Nebuta Matsuri is one of the most famous summer festivals of the Tohoku Region. While huge lanterns with drawings of samurai are lit and carried in procession throughout the city, lively music adds to the festival's fast paced atmosphere. The musical accompaniment is said to have originated to celebrate the triumphant return of victorious samurai. ▶ 115

3. The Winter Festivals of Tohoku

The Kamakura in Yokote
The basin of Yokote was, according to history, where the original inhabitants assimilated into what is considered the Japanese race. During the Edo period, Yokote became a castle town of the Satake Clan. Throughout history, this basin has been the staging ground of many violent disputes and wars. However, today, the area is more commonly known for the location of the peaceful Kamakura Festival, held in February. In this festival, local children make snow houses called kamakura, and then build a fire inside and serve food and a sweet non-alcoholic drink, called amazake. ▶ 117

The Hiburi Kamakura, Fire Festival
Every February on the shores of the Hinokinai River in Kakunodate City, the Hiburi Kamakura Festival takes place. Hiburi, literally means "fire-swinging," and that is what occurs when straw rice sacks are lit on fire and swung at the end of a meter long rope. Through this feat of courage the participants hope for health and well being of their families in the coming year. ▶ 118

4. Minami Aizu

Ouchijuku
Up until the Edo period, Ouchijuku was a lodging town on the road that extended from Aizu Wakamatsu to Nikko. In the Meiji period, a new highway was constructed bypassing the town, and Ouchijuku was forgotten until after the Second World War when its historical significance was rediscovered. As a result, the town retains the traditional architecture of old and has been designated as a Historical Landmark. ▶ 119

Hinoemata Kabuki
In the small village of Hinoemata is the shrine of Atago where twice a year, the Hinoemata Kabuki is performed as it has been for over 200 years. It is said that during the Edo period villagers started this local version of the art by imitating the performances they had seen in the capital. This old and simple form of Kabuki is entirely performed by the villagers. ▶ 120

Tajima Gion Festival
Aizu Tajimamachi holds an annual festival called "Tajima Gion Festival." It was started in the Kamakura period after the Gion Festival of Kyoto. In the festival, a parade of women clad in a bride's costume was added to the annual event in the Edo period. ▶ 121

5. Aizu

Nanokado Hadaka-mairi
The Nanokado Hadaka-mairi of Yanaizumachi in Fukushima Prefecture takes place every January at the Enzoji Temple and is one of the most famous. The hadaka-mairi, or naked festival, takes place in other regions of Japan as well and is based on Buddhist beliefs where men disrobe and perform a ceremony of purification in an energetic manner. When the sound of the temple bell strikes eight o'clock in the evening, the men race up the stone steps to the temple bell where they compete to climb up the gong's rope. The first one to touch the gong will be blessed with honor and happiness for the rest of the year.
▶ 124

Traditional Storehouses
Around Kitakata City, in Fukushima Prefecture, there are over 2,000 storehouses of soybean paste, soy sauce and Japanese sake. Unlike storehouses found in the Kansai and Kanto regions, these buildings, kura is constructed with the forethought of protecting them against heavy winter snows. Kitakata City is extremely active in the preservation of these buildings and when the storehouses are no longer used for storage they are converted to museums and teahouses. In the suburban Sugiyama area, twenty buildings of this architecture remain today.
▶ 122, 123

6. Matsushima

Godaido Hall
Matsushima is one of the "Three Scenic Views" of Japan. After a visit here in the 17th century, the legendary haiku poet Matsuo Basho, avoided making visual descriptions of Matsushima in his poetry and instead wrote of its deeply inspirational qualities: such was the beauty of this place. On one of the small islands that dot the seascape is the Godaido Hall, which has been designated one of Japan's Important Tangible Cultural Properties.
▶ 126

Hote Matsuri
Near Matsushima is the fishing port of Shiogama City where every March the Hote Matsuri takes place. In this festival sixteen parishioners of the Shiogama Temple carry the Great mikoshi, portable shrine, down the 202 stone steps. The festival originated in the 17th century as a symbolic prayer for prevention against fire.
▶ 127

Shiogama Minato Matsuri
In August, Matsushima is host to the Shiogama Minato Matsuri where two local fishing boats decorated with huge colorful banners carry the Great mikoshi, portable shrine through the scenic bay as a way of praying for bountiful catches.
▶ 125

7. Dewa

The Five-Storied Pagoda of Mt. Haguro
In the distant past, Tohoku was home to independent mountain religions drawing in many novice monks. On the way to the religious retreat on the peak of Mt. Haguro is the 29-meter high five-storied pagoda. This pagoda is believed to be the oldest in the Tohoku Region, and legends date it back to the early 10th century. The present pagoda may date back to the 14th century. It is surrounded by giant old cedar trees aged 600 to 1,000 years.
▶ 130

The Traditional Multi-Level Homes of Tamugimata
The village of Tamugimata was once on the road used for pilgrimages from the inland area to the religious sites of the Shonai Plain and was used for the lodging of weary travelers. Because the snowfall is deep and land for building is scarce, a distinct style of architecture to suit these conditions emerged. Rare for traditional Japanese architecture, a three-storied building called kabuto-zukuri, developed. The kabuto-zukuri features a first floor used as a family living space, the second floor for servants and the third floor for raising silkworms and silk weaving. This type of dwelling aided the inhabitants to live comfortably in an otherwise difficult environment.
▶ 128

Kurokawa Noh
In the Dewa Area, the representative form of culture is the Kurokawa Noh plays of Kushibikimachi in Yamagata Prefecture. This Noh theater is known throughout the region for its sophisticated performances, beautiful stage settings and ancient style. Because the Kurokawa Noh has been performed several times each year since the 16th century and preserves cultural traditions, the government has designated it an Important Intangible Cultural Property.
▶ 129

8. Hiraizumi

Hiraizumi is known as the place where after just three generations, the dynasty of Oshu-Fujiwara passed into history. At the beginning of the 12th century, Buddhist architecture was booming and the valuable works of the Heian period are still seen here today.

The Jodo-style Garden of Motsuji Temple
On example of bygone days is the Motsuji Temple, which at one point in time had forty structures and 500 monks in residence. However, even with the power the temple's size garnered, it was lost in the war and today all that remains is the Jodo-style garden. Nonetheless, the garden provides a glimpse of the fine art of natural landscaping.
▶ 131

The Shishi Odori and the Noh-mai Dance in Hiraizumi
The Tohoku Region has a unique custom of using costumes representing deer, wild boar, lions and other animals for kagura, the traditional dance performances. The shishi mai, the popular lion dance, is performed throughout Japan but in Hiraizumi, it is called "Shishi Odori," and the performers wear deer costumes. Other traditional performing arts include the noh-mai dance, which takes place at Chusonji Temple every spring and autumn.
▶ 132, 133

9. Tono

The town of Tono is one of the spots of traditional Japanese folklore, and even today stories of ghosts and other legends about the town abound. The tales include legends about supernatural beings, strange occurrences and the rustic life of villagers. Tono was formed out of the combination of several smaller villages and is known for its pastoric landscape of signposts and watermills. ▶ 136

The Magariya of Tono
At the Denshoen folk park are located the magariya, or L-shaped farm houses unique to Tohoku where both people and horses resided under the same roof but in separated sections. ▶ 134, 135

Hayachine Kagura
Every August, kagura, the traditional dance performance is played at the Hayachine Jinja. It is called "Hayachine Kagura" which was named after the nearby mountains, Mt. Hayachine. The Fast-paced local performing art is believed to have been started by the followers of the mountain religion of "Sangaku Shinko." ▶ 137

10. Kakunodate

Kakunodate is another castle town that has managed to preserve the atmosphere of the Edo period, and most of the former samurai warrior residences have been designated as Important Tangible Cultural Properties. In the Kakunodate area, the architecture is built to withstand the torrid weather in the summers rather than the cold in the winters despite the fact that Kakunodate is snowy country. ▶ 138, 139, 141

Aoyagi House
The Aoyagi family was one of the region's elite samurai families which retained its prominent position for four hundred years. The Aoyagi's family residence offers an example of Kakunodate's elaborate style of architecture for high-ranking samurai. The main gate to the manor has a magnificently decorated roof, which is far and away, the most beautiful in the town. ▶ 140

11. Hirosaki

Hirosaki is the castle town of the Tsugaru Clan, and with 300 years of history, it is commonly referred to as the Kyoto of the Tohoku region. Hirosaki Castle, built in 1611 and rebuilt after it was struck by lightning in 1627, is the home of some 5,000 cherry trees that fill the castle grounds with a profusion of cherry blossoms every late April to early May. Surrounding the castle are many sites designated as Important Cultural Properties such as samurai residences, temples and other historic structures. ▶ 142, 143

Neputa Matsuri
Every August the Neputa Matsuri is held with some sixty ornate Neputa-floats decorated as lanterns and painted with the images of famous samurai warriors are paraded through the city streets. This festival began in 1593 and has remained unchanged since the end of the Edo period in the mid-19th century. ▶ 144

Similar to the Neputa Matsuri is the "Nebuta" Matsuri of Aomori Prefecture. The Nebuta festival is more widely known of the two, even though the drawings on the Neputa Matsuri lanterns are more detailed and ornate.

12. The Natural Beauty of Tohoku

Kuroyu of Nyuto Onsenkyo
In the onsen, hot springs, known as Nyuto Onsenkyo near Lake Tazawa in Akita Prefecture is the secluded resort of Kuroyu. During the autumn, the outdoor bath, with its thatched roof and rock-lined bottom expresses the rustic charm of rural Japan. ▶ 145

Sukayu Onsen
This is one of the famous hot springs of Mt. Hakkoda. Originally the local farmers would come to get relief from its waters, but it is now famous for its sennin buro or thousand-person bath where both men and women can bathe together. ▶ 146

The Oirase River
The Oirase River is the source of the large and beautiful Lake Towada. One stretch of this river is surrounded by a forest of beech trees, and the seasonal landscape is popular with tourists who come to see the lush green of spring and the vibrant colors of autumn. ▶ 147

Hokkaido Region

1. Hakodate

Hakodate is one of the ports first opened after the end of the Edo period. The city was exposed to European influence earlier than other parts of Japan and still retains a foreign atmosphere. Hakodate is famous for its beautiful night scenery which is referred to as a "million-dollar view by night" when looking down from the hilltop. There are many Western-style buildings and a Russian Orthodox Church, a symbolic building, which offers a panoramic view of the port. ▶ 149, 150

2. Sapporo

Sapporo is the capital city of Hokkaido and the seat of the local government. The streets of the city were constructed following western style urban planning. There is a long, green corridor which is the main street, Odori Park, which is decorated with Christmas illuminations in December and becomes a venue for the Sapporo Snow Festival in February. The Sapporo Snow Festival is an annual event featuring a huge exhibition of magnificent snow sculptures. ▶ 150

3. The Ainu

The Ainu, an indigenous people, currently reside in Hokkaido. This indigenous group originally lived in a tribal society with lifestyles based on hunting and fishing, and can trace their origins back to the Jomon people. The Jomons are the prehistoric, stone-age inhabitants of Japan. Until the 10th century, the Ainu lived throughout northern Japan and what is today the Tohoku region, but were gradually pushed out of the area by the Japanese. Since the Meiji period at the end of the 18th century, the Ainu have shifted toward agricultural occupations and have continued to intermarry with the Japanese. Today, there are an estimated 10,000 Ainu living in Hokkaido, still practicing their own unique customs. ▶ 152, 154

Marimo Festival
In October, the Marimo Festival is held in Akan-Kohan, primarily on the edge of Lake Akan, where marimo, a kind of spherical moss is found. The Ainu and the Japanese government have sought to protect the marimo from becoming extinct. The Marimo Festival continues today with traditional Ainu dance to preserve the culture and the nature of the Akan area. The Ainu have traditionally revered marimo as the "spirit" of the lake and the festivities include a ceremony where marimo is returned to the lake. ▶ 153

4. The Nature of Hokkaido

Hokkaido has four national parks where the natural habitat still flourishes on a grand scale. The climate is that of a subarctic zone and the land is covered with virgin forests of Japanese spruce, fir trees, white birch and other types of greenery. This region was not fully opened by the Japanese until 1869 when the central government established kaitakushi, a colonial liaison office in the region. The presence of large ranches and farms gives this vast frontier a "foreign" flavor.

Tancho Cranes in the Kushiro Marshland
The Kushiro Marshland National Park, which encompasses Japan's largest marshland, and the home to some 300 tancho or sacred red-crested cranes, which are designated by the Japanese government as "national monuments." In the summer these cranes live in the marshland, but in the winter they migrate in search of food and move closer to human habitation. Since 1983, conservation efforts for the tancho cranes have gained momentum. ▶ 155

Swans from Siberia
The eastern region of Hokkaido provides a seasonal habitat for swans migrating in the thousands, a scale of migration that is rare for the species. The swans stay to rest here during February and March on their migration from Siberia. ▶ 148

Utoro Port, the Sea of Okhotsk
In the Sea of Okhotsk, off Hokkaido, the winds are bitterly cold and the temperature is severe, often falling ten degrees below Celsius. In early February, drifting ice floes float from the Amur River in Russia to the Seas of Okhotsk. Utoro Port is the southernmost point in the Northern Hemisphere where ice floes of substantial size can be seen. ▶ 156, 157, 158

List of the Plates

Kinki Region
1 Morning view of Yakushiji Temple (Nara City, Nara)

Nara (pp.7–11)
2 The Mantoro lanterns of Kasuga Taisha (Nara City, Nara)
3 Horyuji Temple (Ikarugacho, Nara)
4 The Great Buddha in the Daibutsuden of Todaiji Temple (Nara City, Nara)
5 The Omizutori Fire Festival at Todaiji Temple's Nigatsudo (Nara City, Nara)

Kyoto (pp.12–13)
6 The Aoi Festival (Kyoto City, Kyoto)
7 The Aoi Festival (Kyoto City, Kyoto)
8 The Golden Pavilion (Kinkaku) of Rokuonji Temple (Kyoto City, Kyoto)

Rock Garden Minimalism (pp.14–15)
9 The Daisen-in rock garden at Daitokuji Temple (Kyoto City, Kyoto)
10 The Ryugen-in rock garden at Daitokuji Temple (Kyoto City, Kyoto)
11 The rock garden at Ryoanji Temple (Kyoto City, Kyoto)

Ise (pp.16–17)
12 The Ujibashi Bridge at Ise Jingu Shrine (Ise, Mie)
13 The Nuiho Festival at Jingu Kanda (Ise, Mie)
14 The Otauesai (Rice Planting Festival) at Izawa no Miya (Isobecho, Mie)

Nagahama and Omi Hachiman (p.18)
15 The Old Nishikawa House (Omi Hachiman, Shiga)
16 Children's Kabuki, part of the Hikiyama Festival (Nagahama, Shiga)

Kumano (pp.19–21)
17 The Nachi Falls (Nachikatsuuracho, Wakayama)
18 The three-storied pagoda of the Seigantoji Temple (Nachikatsuuracho, Wakayama)
19 The Nachi no Himatsuri Fire Festival at Nachi Taisha (Nachikatsuuracho, Wakayama)
20 The Oto Festival at Kamikura Jinja (Shingu, Wakayama)

Hokuriku and Chubu Regions
21 An open hearth at Kita House (Nonoichimachi, Ishikawa)

Kanazawa (pp.24–25)
22 Kenrokuen Garden (Kanazawa, Ishikawa)
23 Noh Theater (Kanazawa, Ishikawa)
24 Kita House (Nonoichimachi, Ishikawa)

Fukui (pp.26–27)
25 Moss garden at Heisenji Temple (Katsuyama, Fukui)
26 The Sanmon Gate of Eiheiji Temple (Eiheijicho, Fukui)
27 Lush green at Eiheiji Temple (Eiheijicho, Fukui)

Takayama (pp.28–29)
28 Traditional homes line a street in Takayama (Takayama, Gifu)
29 Cherry trees in bloom line the Miyakawa (Takayama, Gifu)
30 Elaborate karakuri ningyo (puppets) of Takayama Matsuri (Takayama, Gifu)

Traditional-style homes of Hida (pp.30–31)
31 The Old Mishima House (Shokawamura, Gifu)
32 The Yoshijima House (Takayama, Gifu)
33 The Old Kusakabe House (Takayama, Gifu)

Shirakawago (pp.32–33)
34 Koi-nobori (carp streamers) and the Iwase House (Kamitairamura, Toyama)
35 The Doburoku (home-brewed sake) Festival (Shirakawamura, Gifu)
36 A community of gassho-zukuri (hands-clasped-in-prayer) homes (Shirakawamura, Gifu)

Toyamago (pp.34–35)
37 The Shimotsuki Festival (Kamimura, Nagano)
38 The Shimotsuki Festival (Kamimura, Nagano)
39 The Shimotsuki Festival (Kamimura, Nagano)

Kisoji (pp.36–37)
40 Naraijuku (Narakawamura, Nagano)
41 An inn in Otsumago (Nagisomachi, Nagano)
42 An open hearth in Waki-Honjin-Okuya (Nagisomachi, Nagano)

Nagano (p.38)
43 A stone Buddhist image at Manji (Shimosuwamachi, Nagano)
44 Zenkoji Temple (Nagano City, Nagano)

Ogaki (p.39)
45 Setsubun at Hokoin's Hidarime Fudo (Ogaki, Gifu)
46 The Hidarime Fudo Hadaka Matsuri at Hokoin (Ogaki, Gifu)

Lake Hyoko (p.40)
47 Swans on Lake Hyoko (Suibaramachi, Niigata)
48 Swans on Lake Hyoko (Suibaramachi, Niigata)

Jigokudani Onsen (p.41)
49 Monkeys in snow (Yamanouchimachi, Nagano)
50 A monkey in a spa (Yamanouchimachi, Nagano)

Kanto and Tokai Regions
51 The taisai (Great Festival) of Nikko Toshogu (Nikko, Tochigi)

Nikko (pp.44–45)
52 The Three Monkeys of Toshogu (Nikko, Tochigi)
53 The Nikko Sennin Gyoretsu Procession (Nikko, Tochigi)
54 The ornate Yomeimon Gate of Toshogu (Nikko, Tochigi)

Chichibu (pp.46–47)
55 Chichibu Yomatsuri (Night Festival) (Chichibu, Saitama)

Kawagoe (pp.48–49)
56 Kura-zukuri shoka, the traditional fireproof home of a merchant (Kawagoe, Saitama)
57 The 500 Disciples of Buddha, stone images, at Kitain (Kawagoe, Saitama)
58 The Kawagoe Matsuri (Kawagoe, Saitama)

Kamakura (pp.50–51)
59 The Great Buddha at Kamakura (Kamakura, Kanagawa)
60 Tsurugaoka Hachimangu (Kamakura, Kanagawa)
61 Yabusame, mounted archers perform at the Tsurugaoka Hachimangu (Kamakura, Kanagawa)

Mt. Fuji (p.52)
62 Sunset viewed from Lake Motosu-ko (Kamikuishikimura, Yamanashi)
63 Mt. Fuji and Lake Yamanaka (Yamanakakomura, Yamanashi)

The Tokaido (p.53)
64 Ohashiya Lodge at Akasakajuku (Otowacho, Aichi)
65 Ohashiya Lodge at Akasakajuku (Otowacho, Aichi)

Chugoku Region
66 Izumo Taisha (Taishamachi, Shimane)

Miyajima (p.56)
67 The shinba (sacred horse) of Itsukushima Jinja (Miyajimacho, Hiroshima)
68 The five-storied pagoda of Itsukushima Jinja (Miyajimacho, Hiroshima)
69 The otorii (Great Sacred Gate) at Itsukushima Jinja (Miyajimacho, Hiroshima)

Iwakuni (p.57)
70 Kintaikyo Bridge (Iwakuni, Yamaguchi)

Seto Naikai — Japan's Inland Sea (pp.58–59)
71 Dawn breaks over the Inland Sea from Mt. Fudekage (Mihara, Hiroshima)

Merchant Houses in Sanyo (p.60)
72 The Old Katayama House (Nariwacho, Okayama)
73 The Matsuzaka House (Takehara, Hiroshima)

Kurashiki (p.61)
74 A museum dedicated to the building of traditional Japanese storehouses (Kurashiki, Okayama)
75 A scenic canal at Kurashiki (Kurashiki, Okayama)

Tsuwano (p.62)
76 A canal running beside traditional samurai homes (Tsuwanocho, Shimane)
77 The sagi-mai (White Heron Dance) (Tsuwanocho, Shimane)

Himeji (p.63)
78 Himeji Castle colored by the sunset (Himeji, Hyogo)
79 Inside Himeji Castle (Himeji, Hyogo)

Bicchu (p.64)
80 The five-storied pagoda in Kibiji (Soja, Okayama)
81 The night dances of Bicchu (Biseicho, Okayama)

Okayama (p.65)
82 The Hadaka Matsuri at Saidaiji Temple (Okayama City, Okayama)
83 Okayama Castle (Okayama City, Okayama)

Shikoku Region
84 Kazurabashi Bridge (Nishi-iyayamason, Tokushima)

Tokushima (pp.68–69)
85 A performance of Awa Ningyo Joruri (Tokushima City, Tokushima)
86 A performance at Jurobe no Yashiki (Tokushima City, Tokushima)
87 The Awa-odori dance (Tokushima City, Tokushima)

Kagawa (pp.70–71)
88 Ema (votive tablets) at the Emado, Kotohiragu Shrine (Kotohiracho, Kagawa)
89 An engineering marvel, the Seto Ohashi Bridge (Sakaide, Kagawa)
90 Marugame Castle (Marugame, Kagawa)
91 Ritsurin Park (Takamatsu, Kagawa)

Uchiko (p.72)
92 Kami-Haga-tei (Uchikocho, Ehime)
93 Latticework at Hon-Haga-tei (Uchikocho, Ehime)
94 The Uchiko-za Theater (Uchikocho, Ehime)

Matsuyama (p.73)
95 Dogo Onsen (Matsuyama, Ehime)

Kyushu and Okinawa Regions
96 The stern face of the Usuki Stone Buddha (Usuki, Oita)

Nagasaki (p.76)
97 The Peiron Boat Race (Nagasaki City, Nagasaki)
98 Oura Tenshudo (Nagasaki City, Nagasaki)
99 Nagasaki at dusk (Nagasaki City, Nagasaki)

Sakurajima (p.77)
100 A volcanic eruption at Sakurajima (Kagoshima City, Kagoshima)

Obi (p.78)
101 Obi Castle (Nichinan, Miyazaki)
102 A flume of an old samurai residence (Nichinan, Miyazaki)

Chiran (p.79)
103 An old samurai residence (Chirancho, Kagoshima)
104 An old samurai residence (Chirancho, Kagoshima)

Aso (p.80)
105 The Onda Matsuri (planting festival) of Aso Jinja (Ichinomiyamachi, Kumamoto)
106 The Onda Matsuri (planting festival) of Aso Jinja (Ichinomiyamachi, Kumamoto)

Shiromi (p.81)
107 A Shiromi Kagura performance (Saito, Miyazaki)

Okinawa (pp.82–83)
108 The sun goes down on Nagura Bay (Ishigakijima, Okinawa)
109 Traditional homes of Taketomijima (Taketomijima, Okinawa)
110 The Tanetorisai (Taketomijima, Okinawa)

Tohoku Region
111 Harvested rice (Zao, Yamagata)

The Summer Festivals of Tohoku (pp.86–90)
112 The Nishimonai Bon Odori dance (Ugomachi, Akita)
113 A Tanabata Picture lantern (Yuzawa, Akita)
114 The Nishimonai Bon Odori dance (Ugomachi, Akita)
115 Aomori's Nebuta Matsuri (Aomori City, Aomori)
116 Great towers of lanterns at Akita's Kanto Matsuri (Akita City, Akita)

The Winter Festivals of Tohoku (p.91)
117 Kamakura, small snow scene (Yokote, Akita)
118 Hiburi Kamakura, Fire Festival (Kakunodatemachi, Akita)

Minami Aizu (pp.92–93)
119 A row of thatched houses in Ouchijuku (Ouchijuku, Fukushima)
120 Hinoemata Kabuki (Hinoematamura, Fukushima)
121 Tajima Gion Festival (Tajimamachi, Fukushima)

Aizu (pp.94–95)
122 A farmhouse with a traditional storehouse in Sugiyama District (Kitakata, Fukushima)
123 A farmhouse with a traditional storehouse in Sugiyama District (Kitakata, Fukushima)
124 The Nanokado Hadaka-mairi (Yanaizumachi, Fukushima)

Matsushima (pp.96–97)
125 A festive ship in the Shiogama Port Festival (Shiogama, Miyagi)
126 Matsushima's Godaido Hall (Matsushimacho, Miyagi)
127 A shrine in the Hote Matsuri (Shiogama, Miyagi)

Dewa (pp.98–99)
128 The villager and the multi-level homes of Tamugimata (Kushibikimachi, Yamagata)
129 Kurokawa Noh performed at Kushibikimachi (Kushibikimachi, Yamagata)
130 The five-storied pagoda of Mt. Haguro (Haguromachi, Yamagata)

Hiraizumi (pp.100–101)
131 The Jodo-style garden of Motsuji Temple (Hiraizumicho, Iwate)
132 The noh-mai dance of Chusonji Temple (Hiraizumicho, Iwate)
133 The Shishi Odori (Hiraizumicho, Iwate)

Tono (pp.102–103)
134 A farmhorse (Tono, Iwate)
135 A traditional magariya (Tono, Iwate)
136 Remains of the Hayachine pilgrimage trail (Tono, Iwate)
137 Hayachine Kagura, traditional entertainment (Ohasamamachi, Iwate)

Kakunodate (pp.104–105)
138 The storehouse of a traditional warrior's residence (Kakunodatemachi, Akita)
139 A traditional warrior's home (Kakunodatemachi, Akita)
140 The front gate of the Aoyagi House (Kakunodatemachi, Akita)
141 A snowy street in front of a traditional warrior's house (Kakunodatemachi, Akita)

Hirosaki (pp.106–107)
142 The 500 wooden disciples of Buddha at Choshoji Temple (Hirosaki, Aomori)
143 Hirosaki Castle and cherry trees in bloom (Hirosaki, Aomori)
144 An ornate float in the Neputa Matsuri (Hirosaki, Aomori)

The Natural Beauty of Tohoku (pp.108–109)
145 Kuroyu of Nyuto Onsenkyo (Tazawakomachi, Akita)
146 Sukayu Onsen (Mt. Hakkoda, Aomori)
147 The beautiful Oirase River (Towadakomachi, Aomori)

Hokkaido Region
148 Swans at Akan National Park (Akan National Park, Hokkaido)

Hakodate (p.112)
149 A Russian Orthodox Church (Hakodate, Hokkaido)
150 Night view of Hakodate (Hakodate, Hokkaido)

Sapporo (p.113)
151 Christmas at Odori Park (Sapporo, Hokkaido)

Ainu (pp.114–115)
152 Lake Onneto (Akan National Park, Hokkaido)
153 The Marimo Festival (Akancho, Hokkaido)
154 Ainu people (Akancho, Hokkaido)

A Hokkaido Winter Scene (pp.116–120)
155 Tancho cranes in mating dance (Tsuruimura, Hokkaido)
156 Ice floes off the Sea of Okhotsk (Utoro, Hokkaido)
157 Sunset in Okhotsk (Utoro, Hokkaido)
158 Port Utoro in winter (Utoro, Hokkaido)

Japan Rediscovered
日本のこころ

2008年3月29日　第1刷発行
2013年2月26日　第2刷発行

著　者　　植村　正春

発行者　　浦　晋亮

発行所　　IBC パブリッシング株式会社
　　　　　〒162-0804 東京都新宿区中里町29番3号　菱秀神楽坂ビル9F
　　　　　Tel. 03-3513-4511　Fax. 03-3513-4512
　　　　　www.ibcpub.co.jp

カバーデザイン　　室伏　宏保（アイアンドアイ）

本文レイアウト　　岡崎　健二

印刷所　　株式会社カシヨ

© Masaharu Uemura 2008
© IBC Publishing, Inc. 2008

落丁本・乱丁本は、小社宛にお送りください。送料小社負担にてお取り替えいたします。
本書の無断複写（コピー）は著作権法上での例外を除き禁じられています。

Printed in Japan
ISBN 978-4-89684-679-9